Die Neatly

How to Live a Financially Meaningful Life
by Preparing for The Inevitable

Jim Lusk, CFP®, CLU®, ChFC®, MEd

Jim Lusk

Spokane, WA

D1533923

Jim Lusk
Spokane, WA

www.RetirementNationwide.com

Ordering Information:
Quantity sales. Special discounts may be available on quantity purchases by corporations, associations, and others. For details, jim@retirementnationwide.com.

Die Neatly
Jim Lusk —1st ed.
ISBN 978-0-578-70945-1

Disclaimer

This book is a teaching tool and is for educational purposes only. Past performance, stories, and numbers cited do not guarantee future results, and the views expressed in it are mine alone. While I freely share my knowledge throughout this book, and share what has worked for me, I can't guarantee you (or anyone) specific results from reading this (or any) book. Because of that, neither myself nor the publisher accepts any liability in any form as a result of reading this book.

Now, with that being shared, know this: I have faith in you, and all people that, with the right information, help, and action you can accomplish your financial goals and dreams. Enjoy the book!

Table of Contents

To my wife Debbie, daughters Jaimie and Jodi, son-in-law Tom, and my three awesome grandchildren: Dinah, Ezekiel, and Enoch (and future children and spouses of them).

FORWARD

In *Die Neatly,* Jim Lusk uses timeless, authentic and, at times, personally vulnerable stories to teach the importance of dealing with the uncertainties of life in a proactive and "defensive" way. Whether it's dying too soon, suffering a disability, enduring a long-term care event, or warding off lawsuits, Jim's "Defensive Financial Planning" approach shines a light on the often unheralded, but nonetheless critical, components of a sound financial plan.

This book is an important reminder that creating an enduring financial roadmap is about more than racking up huge returns in your retirement portfolio. Jim argues that the pursuit of an offensive financial strategy without the crucial underpinnings of a good defensive plan will make your eventual demise anything but "neat" for your heirs who are left holding the bag.

Jim has spent the last four decades implementing his "Defensive Financial Planning" system in the lives of his clients. His insight and wisdom leaps off the page and reminds you of the importance of having an experienced guide to help navigate the pitfalls that stand between you and your financial goals and aspirations.

-David McKnight, author of *The Power of Zero*

PREFACE

A Long Time Coming

As a 65-year-old financial planner with over 37 years of experience in the retirement and estate planning arena, I've helped thousands of clients and advisers turn their desires into wise designs. Throughout my years, I've paid out numerous death claims (from insurance companies, pensions, and IRAs), consoled widows/widowers, and helped advisors do the same. It's been a gratifying career, but it all began quite humbly with wise counsel in my early years.

When I started as a young 28-year-old agent in the life insurance business, my mentor and friend, Jim Bockemuehl, pleaded with me, "don't be hypocritical." He instilled the truth in me that you have to "own what you sell" and "practice what you preach." Thus, from the very start I spent serious time and money planning for the possibility of my early demise. I bought bunches of life insurance and created a will to ensure my young, beautiful wife and two precious preschool daughters would be taken care of when death came for me, whether early or late.

By God's grace, death hasn't come early for me, and in a few short years I'll reach 40 years since I first began planning for my own "inevitable occurrence" of death (more on that in Chapter 3). Over all these years I've continued to hone my personal planning, even changing my will over four times in the past 10 years because life keeps changing.

What has changed? For starters, my precious girls are now fully-grown adults (but still precious). My wife and I, sadly, aren't quite so young anymore (but she's still beautiful). Doesn't time fly by? Given this reality, updates have been necessary because my vision has expanded beyond my fledgling family to the generations to come. Now I want to have enough assets and life insurance to guarantee a quality lifestyle for my grandchildren and beyond. I also have a plan to leave 10% of my estate to charity, and I hope I can inspire many others to also decide to "tithe their estate" (see Chapter 10).

Returning to my aforementioned decades of planning, some might say all my effort hasn't done much for me (since I'm still alive and occasionally kicking), but I'm here to tell you how very wrong that notion is indeed. Despite my family not yet tapping into the financial benefit of my after-death arrangements (because I'm not dead!), my planning has accrued for me a truly tremendous (and unexpected) benefit for all these past years.

Through planning, there's been a peace of mind given to me that has washed away much of the strain I didn't even realize I was under. Instead of back-of-the-mind "what if *this* happens!" or "how will my family survive?" whispers muddling my mind, I've experienced such a cleansing clarity of purpose. Maybe this sounds weird, but facing and wisely planning for my death over these many years has empowered me to live more genuinely and abundantly, even purely.

To put it simply, it feels so darn great knowing my family will be financially okay in the event of my premature death. My motivation for writing this book is to share this fantastic feeling that has flourished in me ever since the age of 28. If you don't know the sensation yourself, I want you, also, to feel like I do and walk in the same unforeseen blessing of wise Defensive Financial Planning.

So, please come along with me as we explore together what it means to prepare and plan in order to "die neatly."

An Introduction to "Dying Neatly"

As you read this book, I want you to feel the safety of having a great plan, not to help you get rich, but to make sure your family is "OK" financially if you die prematurely. I also want you to think about your dreams and goals and ask yourself, "what could keep these plans from happening, and can I or should I protect against those losses?"

Why? *Because the reality is, if you have a plan, you can live a freer life.* You've removed a lot of the worries about the big "what ifs" (premature death, disability and long-term care). Your investments may or may not work as planned, but "Defensive Financial Planning" is about transferring risk "for pennies on the dollar" and having a self-completion plan when you're not here to see it through.

I want you to picture driving on a steep mountain road with no guardrails. How fast would you go? Would you consider turning back? Do you want to remove or transfer some of that risk? I would like for you to think about this book as helping you set up "guardrails" on that road so you can enjoy the ride, but with protection.

How about the title: *DIE NEATLY?* My goal is to help you embrace the inevitable, death, so you can live an amazing life *now*. If it happens too soon, use these tools and plans available so that you and your family/business won't suffer financially too. During almost forty years of advising clients, I have found that the gross majority have no will or trust completed. One of my first recommendations is for them to meet with an attorney who can help crystallize their estate plan, so the State doesn't do it for you. Most people procrastinate this estate planning process, because of "the river in Egypt" - DENIAL. One of the most googled phrases during this recent Covid-19 Pandemic is "life insurance." We are realizing as a society that we are all perishable and death can come quickly.

This is not to scare you. It's about living a great life, because you've taken time to plan for potential catastrophic losses. I want to share my story, because I too had to be SOLD to get a will and trust done for my young family forty years ago. I certainly didn't want to buy more life insurance, and I was terrible at saving money. But I was coachable, respected my advisors, and realized I'd be better off later by planning early.

What about if you're young and just getting a family started and say, "I have no money yet?" I want you to know that you're probably worth millions of dollars. (Google: Human Life Value). As you make money; save some first, spend some, give some to charity, but also allocate funds to protect your MONEY MACHINE if it breaks down too soon. My hope is that you live a long-blessed life, but the timing of when you leave this earth is not up to me or you...only God knows.

It is my sincere desire that you will find great value in studying this book and that you gain enough wisdom to motivate you and others to make sound financial decisions in order to DIE NEATLY.

CHAPTER 1

Three Possibilities – Best, Worst, and Take What Comes

Defensive Financial Planning requires healthy mental thinking. Before the contracts and signatures, a person must reach a level of awareness of certain realities and uncertainties of life. So, before diving into the "die neatly" meat, let me whet your appetite with a philosophical starter called "my philosophy of three possibilities." Before sharing the exact recipe, let me tell you a story of my daughter, an audition, and old Saint Nick.

In 1991, when my oldest daughter, Jaimie, was 12 years old, she came home from school one day all forlorn. I asked her what was wrong, and her response was, "Life is not fair, guys always get the best deals!" Wow, I thought. What did she mean and where was this coming from?

Soon I learned that at her school there was a play called "Shaping Up Santa" with a funny premise about Santa getting sent to a fitness center to lose some weight. As far as elementary school plays go, it was cute and very creative. Jaimie's problem was that Santa had fifty lines, a couple of dance routines, and a singing solo, but Mrs. Clause had only thirty lines and no solo. So, the best part was for guys only since, in her mind, Jaimie couldn't be Santa because she was a girl.

After listening to her, I said, "Why not try out for Santa? All of you are 12-year-olds and can manage to sound and look about the same. Put your long hair in a ponytail and no one will know. If the teacher is a chauvinist and says, 'It's a boy's part,' we'll go to the principal and even the school board to challenge it. What do you say?"

She lit up and said, "Let's go for it!" In response to her enthusiasm I took this opportunity to guide her through "my philosophy of three possibilities" that I've preached for years:

1. **Hope for the Best.** – Try to get the best outcome possible.

2. **Prepare for the Worst.** – If you don't get it, what's your plan?

3. **Take what Comes with Gratitude.** – Be content; you may have little control.

Now our philosophy of "hope for the best" doesn't mean you always get the best. Jaimie decided to hope for the best and try out for a "male role," but that didn't mean she would get the main part. She still had to have a better audition than her classmates, and that required much dedication and discipline.

The second point, prepare for the worst, means thinking through possible outcomes. In Jaimie's case, we discussed the ramifications of not getting the Santa role. If she didn't get it because someone else was better, then that's reasonable, but what would happen if she decides to challenge her teacher or other authorities if she felt the part wasn't given to her due to her gender? There could be retaliation, hard or hurt feelings, and frustrations. It's wise to be prepared for the worst, even while hoping for the best.

After this discussion, she was prepared to do the audition and accept the consequences, which led to "take what comes." If we try hard and do our best, things still may not go our way. Accept with gratitude what comes to us with the knowledge that we did all we could. For those of us who believe in God, maybe God's will is that sometimes we don't get what we want (or even much of the time). By accepting the outcome, we protect ourselves from getting stuck in bitterness and resentment. We are positioned to begin anew the cycle of hoping, preparing, and taking what comes.

Wrapping up Jaimie's story, thankfully, there's a happy ending. Jaimie got the Santa part and entertained the audience with passion, convincing us all that she truly was Santa. Over the rest of her childhood years Jaimie went on to hope for the best, prepare for the worst, and take what comes with gratitude.

From this solid foundation, she later graduated from the Naval Academy and served as a Marine Corps officer in Kuwait. Today she holds a Doctorate of Psychology and works with struggling Veterans as a Post-Traumatic Stress Disorder (PTSD) expert. She's passionate about helping others to emotionally and psychologically heal, and I couldn't be prouder!

Your life is a fragile, perishable time on earth. Ben Feldman (known as the greatest life insurance agent ever[1]) said, "We're all one heartbeat from eternity, but we don't know which one. A momentary lapse on the highway, a body temperature change of 6 degrees either way, and we're not here any longer. Let me ask you, what's your plan?"

---

[1] Life of a Salesman. The New York Times.
https://www.nytimes.com/1978/04/02/archives/life-of-a-salesman-life.html

In the spirit of Ben, let me turn this question to you: what is your personal plan? To help you answer this question, let us look beyond "Shaping Up Santa," and apply my philosophy of three possibilities to the concept of "dying neatly."

1. **Hope for the Best.** We all want to live a long, happy, and quality life. I want to live beyond age 90 with no dementia so I can remember and maintain relationships with those I love. I also want my investments to always go up in value and have my money outlast me. But I still...

2. **Prepare for the Worst.** The worst for most people is dying prematurely before they accomplish their goals. They might pass on far too young and before many assets could be built up for their family. Sometimes disability or chronic conditions happen before death resulting in a poor "quality of life" with too much pain, poor mobility, and mental illness. To make matters worse, this often means that your loved ones lose or diminish your income and spend an exorbitant amount of time and money caring for you.

3. **Take what Comes with Gratitude.** Are you prepared to deal with the problems outlined above? I've had people say to me "If I am gone it won't be my problem!" But your family should still be

important to you even after your death, and the problems left upon surviving loved ones could be greatly reduced or even eliminated with a little planning. Mentally accepting and being grateful to "take what comes" will feel very stressful without a plan. Taking the time to create a "defensive financial plan" (Chapter 2) will give you a "peace of mind" that will allow you to live more freely and even take more courageous risks, if desired.

My wife has never had a speeding ticket in almost fifty years of driving, and she is always reminding me to slow down. To her, the most frustrating way for me to die would be a "stupid car wreck," and this is a real fear for her and countless others. In my case, I admit I drive too fast, distracted and sometimes struggle with aggressive tendencies. I'm just glad I don't drink, or I'd probably not be here, but I still have to constantly remind myself to slow down to reduce the odds of that "stupid car wreck" happening.

However, a person with a perfect driving record could still be T-boned by a negligent or drunk driver and killed. So, you never know what life will throw you, but you can't live in fear or none of us would ever leave the house. So, it does us much good to "hope for the best," even in the midst of uncertainty.

Let me clarify that when I say, "take what comes," I mean: *be willing to have your family deal with the consequences of your planning (or lack thereof)*. Sure, you might die prematurely and at that point you personally are free from making decisions, but now your loved ones are left to make complicated decisions without your guidance (and income). Is that really what you want?

Over thirty years ago I went to an estate planning meeting, and a middle-aged attorney giving a presentation asked, "Could someone please define 'estate planning?'" There were over a hundred professionals in the room including CPAs, attorneys, CLU®s, and bank trust officers. A young attorney in the front row answered, "It is the transfer of your assets upon your demise to the appropriate people at the appropriate time through wills and trusts." I thought that answer sounded great, but our presenter said, "No," and he went to the board and wrote:

ESTATE PLANNING = DIE NEATLY

This definition got a chuckle from the crowd, and then he asked, "With that in mind, who needs an estate plan? Pretty much everyone!" Therefore, this book is not just for the wealthy—it's for the majority, because the majority of people want to live a good, long life that ends well. To have such a life requires effort and planning!

Although the estate attorney was focusing on wills and trusts, I'm taking the idea of "dying neatly" and expanding it to cover a full range of risks, because even with the best planning you often can't control life. Catastrophes will come, so you must prepare for the worst by "stress testing" your future life to manage risks like premature death, disability, and the need for long-term care.

Just like my daughter Jaimie did all she could to win the role of Santa all those years back, only once you have done your part can you then "take what comes with gratitude," knowing you've done all you can. Through planning, you will have a *peace of mind* knowing that if one of those "ugly events" happens, your family will still be okay!

First comes mental awareness through a clear view of reality and then comes the executing of a wise strategy for your specific life situation. Which leads us into the meat of the preparation, what I call "Defensive Financial Planning."

CHAPTER 2

Defensive Financial Planning – Defense Wins Championships

Now that we're mentally engaged through our philosophy of three possibilities, let's use a sports analogy to discuss the financial world in terms of "offense" and "defense." The offense part is the glamorous smatter like hot investment tips, wealth accumulation, etc. Far too many financial planners focus just in this realm. I say this because without a strong defense you have no foundation to build an offense.

The defense part is about managing the risks that can happen to you like premature death, disability, and long-term care needs. Maybe risk management isn't flashy, but what good is wealth if you haven't planned for your health? Therefore, the cornerstone of dying neatly is Defensive Financial Planning. Let me further explain, starting with a personal sports-related story.

Around twenty years ago I was a manager with a large mutual life insurance company, and I had a young agent who was All-PAC-8 (now PAC-12) while he played wide receiver at the University of Oregon. After three years of playing professional football in CFL, he began working for our firm. We were discussing prospects and I encouraged him to have lunch with me and the head coach from the University of Oregon. Though my new agent was sure that this coach was taken care of, he set up a meeting with my urging.

At lunch, after initial pleasantries, the coach looked at me and said, "You wouldn't be here if it weren't for him (referring to my star recruit)."

"I am okay with that if you are," I half-joked. Then I volunteered to sit in another booth and have lunch alone.

He responded with, "No, that's okay, let's have lunch."

We continued to talk, and he said that he had been working with the same financial planner for 20 years and was very pleased with his work. He had no desire to "move" any money. This was the first time that I introduced the "football concept" and I drew it out on a piece of paper like this:

DIAGRAM: Financial Planning Football

I admitted to this middle-aged college coach that his financial planner was probably really good at "offense" (investments, tax shelters, and wealth accumulation), but I said, "We are applying for the job of being the 'defensive coordinators' of your financial team." You'll always be the head coach.

After discussing his "defense" it turned out that he had an outdated will, very little life insurance, and no long-term care insurance. We were able to put together a solid "defensive retirement plan" that he and his wife loved. He ended up with more expertise on his financial planning "team." We respected his investment advisor (offensive coordinator) and vice versa. We also worked with other members of the coaching staff and had a lot of fun over the next few years.

Why Defense?

In this highly specialized world, we need more "defensive specialists." It is harder psychologically because you have to discuss emotionally draining subjects like premature death, disability, dementia, and other unpleasant topics. People would rather discuss compounding interest, wealth accumulation, investments, and money.

As a result, we have less than half of the advisors in this industry than we did thirty years ago, and the average age is over 55. Yet, the demand for "defensive specialists" has risen. Where are all of the millennials and gen-Xers? How about more women and minorities? If you're looking for a career change, take a serious look at this honorable profession. It's highly rewarding financially, psychologically, and even spiritually.

If you like sports you probably know the saying "offense scores points, defense wins championships." Think about the history of professional football and this proves true. In the 2018 Super Bowl, the New England Patriots beat the Los Angeles Rams 13-3—the lowest scoring Super Bowl in history. The score was only 3-3 at halftime! The Rams averaged 30 points a game coming into the championship, but New England's defense was well fortified. They were prepared for the worst and won!

Baseball, my favorite sport, boasts some of the most incredible skills in the form of pitching. The starters and relief pitchers of the teams that are winning are able to shut down the star Major League hitters! As an aside, 2019 Major League Baseball set the homerun record and runs per game record (offense) but the World Series championship was determined by pitching (defense).

So, what is the connection between sports and your financial well-being (especially if you couldn't care less about sports)? Just like a team of awesome offense getting shut down, your total financial well-being can be shut down without proper defensive planning.

Although I am a Certified Financial Planner (CFP®) and a long-time member of the NAIFA (National Association of Insurance and Financial Advisors), I tell many associates that I don't just want to be—like most CFP®s—in the "moving and storage" business. By that I mean that I don't just want to invest people's money, get them a little higher yield and diversification, charge them a 1% annual fee, and not even deal with risk management.

What are some of the risks? Dying too soon, becoming disabled so income can't be earned (or earned as efficiently as before), having to go into a nursing home or pay for homecare, being sued for hundreds of thousands of dollars, car accidents with major damage not covered by insurance.

There are plenty more risks that all need to be managed. Otherwise, even when working with the best money manager in the world, most of your future wealth can be lost in an instant if you don't have a good defensive retirement plan. A great investment portfolio is not enough to protect a family from the premature death of a wage earner (Chapter 3) or a devastating family disability (Chapter 11).

Don't fire your advisor. But, if he/she doesn't have expertise in this area, hire a "defensive coordinator" to handle your risk management and let your advisor stay in his or her level of expertise as your "offensive coordinator." Never forget that you should be the "head coach," the one who makes the ultimate decisions and monitors the whole "game of life."

There is a great saying:

"People don't plan to fail. They fail to plan."

This saying works for offense and defense. Plan your life and work your plan!

You may be familiar with the work of Dr. Abraham Maslow, the man who created a visual "hierarchy of needs," theorizing that we cannot exist in a higher level until we are comfortable in the level below. One cannot feel secure while struggling to have enough food, and a feeling of belonging cannot happen until one feels secure, and so on. Only then can a person reach "self-actualization."

DIAGRAM: Maslow's Hierarchy of Needs

Self-actualization
desire to become the most that one can be

Esteem
respect, self-esteem, status, recognition, strength, freedom

Love and belonging
friendship, intimacy, family, sense of connection

Safety needs
personal security, employment, resources, health, property

Physiological needs
air, water, food, shelter, sleep, clothing, reproduction

I believe Maslow's "hierarchy of needs" concept can be applied to your financial life. The most fundamental need for money is for survival. You strive to get a job or career to make sure that the daily necessities of food and shelter (and other bills) are covered as the foundation. Once survival is attained, security can be built up, which financially means building up your savings for the uncertain future.

The next financial need affords us proactive protection from the aforementioned uncertain future. With survival and security established, you are empowered to formulate "risk management" strategies to offset potential catastrophic risks. Enter in insurance: car insurance, home insurance, health insurance, liability insurance, disability insurance, long-term care insurance, and, of course, life insurance (the "end game" insurance). (I tell people while many advisors shy away from life insurance, I embrace it as my calling.)

The three steps of survival, security, and catastrophe planning form my triumvirate (trio) of Defensive Financial Planning. These building blocks may not be as flashy as the higher needs, but without them you and your family are just a step away from being decimated.

See the following diagram, which breaks down our financial needs, akin to Maslow.

DIAGRAM: Jim's Hierarchy of Financial Needs

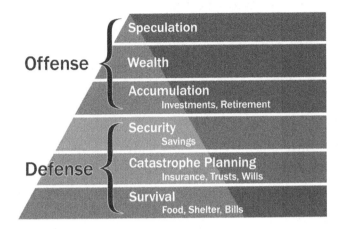

Many people bypass building their financial foundation because they strongly desire to accumulate wealth first. We often hear (and maybe have even said) "I'm going to be rich!" or "don't miss out on this amazing investment!" Rarely does someone say a much wiser aspiration such as "I'm going to prudently insure my family against catastrophe." This last one may not be as exciting of a headline, but which sentiment seems most sensible to you?

Maslow instructs us that knowledge, ability, and beauty can't be truly appreciated without nourishment and protection and basic belonging. Likewise, lucrative investment opportunities and luxury purchases should only be realized when we have a stable foundation set up to support our higher financial aspirations.

Let me repeat myself: A great investment portfolio is not enough to protect a family from the premature death of a wage earner or a devastating *family disability*. Rather, adequately planning against catastrophes (after establishing survival and security) is what allows us to properly engage in the realm of "offensive planning."

Maybe we'll end up rich or maybe we won't, but we can end up in a good place financially if we diligently attend to our most basic "defensive" financial needs. I believe Maslow would agree: there is no good life without a good foundation. The same goes with our financial lives. "Offense" may be flashy but "defense" wins championships in sports and also "wins" your family's future.

After the physiological needs are met, a security strategy should be in place to continue meeting physiological needs—ultimately to prevent poverty—in an unfortunate event. Only then, with excess money, can a person safely move up the financial hierarchy. The goal shouldn't be an outlandish pursuit to join the wealthiest 1%. The goal should be to create a stable quality of life, and that goal can only happen with a secure foundation. In other words, most people need to build a better "defense" before starting an aggressive pursuit of wealth (offensive planning). This defensive mindset is where most people's money and focus should lie.

If you really want financial success and peace of mind, you need a GREAT plan for safety and security (insurance). Accumulating wealth is wonderful, but it ought to be built gradually upon the solid foundation of security. You may never get rich quickly, but you won't ever be poor!

This "poverty prevention plan" is the benefit of Defensive Financial Planning. It is like building a home. A solid foundation remains even after a storm has blown the walls. The Bible teaches us this saying: "A house built on sand will not stand." Preventing the crumbling of your financial life is what we're talking about. Sure, things like concrete slabs, steel reinforcements, and wooden beams may not be as flashy as custom cabinetry and fine furnishings, but it's these basics that allow the fancier things in your life to shine.

In other words, your financial goal is to "build foundations, not chandeliers." Everybody loves a sparkling chandelier, but have you ever seen one come crashing down? Such is the shattering fate of those who invest in luxury products before putting in place a proper "poverty prevention plan." Consider the following diagram.

DIAGRAM: Building a Financial Home

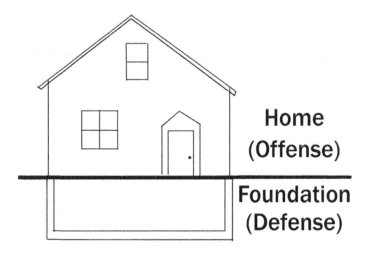

Home
(Offense)

Foundation
(Defense)

Think about building a home. You need to start with a solid, concrete foundation and then build the home. If the foundation cracks it may leak or create moisture, mold, and other undesirable health risks. If it shifts, the whole house may become unstable.

As you build your "financial house," build a solid foundation with emphasis on "defensive planning" (risk management) so that if the house is destroyed by fire, storms, etc. (premature death, disability, etc.), you (or your loved ones) can rebuild the house on the same foundation.

Defensive Financial Planning is all about setting up a strong defense to enable us to live our lives from a place of planned *peace of mind.* There's a time for offensive financial maneuvers to meet our desires for success and wealth, but we must have a stable plan to fall back upon when times get rough. Life *will* get rough for all of us. Many won't ever live in luxury, but even the wealthy have to contend with hardships. The biggest, most certain hardship of all is the subject of our next chapter.

CHAPTER 3

Death – The Inevitable Occurrence

"We're all one heartbeat from eternity, we don't know which one. A momentary lapse on the highway, a body temperature change 6-7 degrees either way and we're not here. Let me ask you, what's your plan?" - Ben Feldman

So far we've covered my philosophy of three possibilities and how it intersects with the critical importance of Defensive Financial Planning. Now it is time to address the most persistent reality each and every one of us faces: all those blessed with life shall also experience death. Given this book's title, it only makes sense that death—the inevitable occurrence—is where we begin forming our reality-based plan to "die neatly." So, let's dive in.

The pastor of my church in Eugene, Oregon back in the 1990s once said, "Mortality rates have hovered around 100% for years." When I first heard this, I burst out laughing along with a few others in the congregation, but some didn't get it. "Hovered" tipped it for me: a 100% chance means you've got the most laser-precise "hover" imaginable. Nobody's going to slip by or dip past death.

I was a math major in college and I love statistics. Many people invent statistics and say things like "90% of people..." or "75% of Americans..." When I hear such pronouncements, I'm always curious about how the data was obtained. I'm reminded of a saying from my engineering professor back in 1975: "Figures don't lie; liars just figure." (He also said 80% of statistics are made up on the spot.)

Statistical diatribe aside, the "100% death rule" is one statistic that is always true. Data from a massive cross-section over thousands and thousands of years has proven that 100% of people will die. How profound is that? As a faith side note (see Chapter 13), Physically speaking, there is no plan. There is merely the 100% certainty that you *will* die. The million-dollar question is "when?"

Unfortunately, death is almost always an uninvited guest, arriving at an unknowable time for most people. Given that death is inevitable, but its timing is virtually unknowable, it is essential that we all plan as much as possible within the constraints that limit us all. In this book I present facts and probabilities meant to give us motivation to stop procrastinating our planning or deny the reality of death (see the next chapter). The inescapable truth is death could happen any time to any of us, but can we lessen the blow? Yes, we can through risk management! Let me explain.

Think about what we worry about most frequently in life. Our worries may focus on natural disasters, our houses being burglarized, car crashes, and so on. We can worry and fret so much that we turn remote possibilities into likely probabilities in our minds. Statistically speaking, though, consider the possibility of our fears occurring. Most of these events will hopefully never (or very infrequently) come to fruition, but most of us buy insurance anyway to mitigate the risk of these incidents.

And yet, as already established, the one certain probability is death. Understand that your risk of death is 100%. Death ought to be thought about, talked about, and planned for by the same percentage of people that it affects: 100% of us. As to why people don't think more about their own deaths, we'll discuss this further in Chapter 4 (denial!).

Risk management is what many insurance companies deal with. Your property and casualty (P&C) agent will insure against property damage and physical injuries related to your home, car, personal property, and so on. We're talking about events like fires, floods, hurricanes, tornados, car crashes, accidents at home, etc. This insurance protects you from financial liability that can cause tens of thousands of dollars in damage. Does this mean that you should insure against all said risks? To answer this question, let's consider the risk using a snow blower as an example.

A while back I bought a snow blower for $700, and I was given the option to pay another $150 for a "maintenance agreement" with a 2-year unlimited warranty for all parts and labor. Should I buy the warranty? Well, if this brand-new snow blower breaks down, it is a bummer, but a $700 risk is not worth a $150 insurance (warranty) cost for two reasons. First, the insurance costs over 20% of the item, itself, which is a large percentage. Second, on the very unlikely chance the snow blower does break, I could buy another one without ruining my lifestyle. Therefore, my belief is that you only insure against catastrophic losses, so be careful you're not electing to insure non-catastrophic events.

Making correct choices is what risk management is about. It is planning and choosing which risks to absorb or "self-insure" and which ones to pay premiums to an insurance company to transfer the risk to them. Car insurance for liability is mandatory and ought to be. Imagine getting T-boned by someone with no liability insurance. Collision and comprehensive are optional (unless you finance the vehicle and the lender is protecting their asset by requiring coverages). However, a 10-year-old car might be "liability only" because you can just buy another pre-owned car if it's totaled and your fault.

Suppose you buy a $60,000 truck and have full coverage because you financed it at zero interest for 36 months. After 36 months it is paid off but has 70,000 miles and is only worth $20,000. At that point, why not absorb the "collision risk" and pay liability only? Each year you pay the same premiums to insure a decreasing value asset. Study this—don't automatically pay for comprehensive car insurance on older vehicles.

Speaking of vehicles, "maintenance agreements" are some of the most profitable insurances in America because the payouts are so small compared to the premiums. For example, when you buy a new car, the dealer may tempt you with sweet-sounding "bumper to bumper" insurance coverage, but you end up paying up front for minor repairs that could be easily paid out-of-pocket years down the road.

I believe you need to avoid these maintenance agreements, and in regard to smaller depreciating purchases (consumer electronics), assume the risk yourself. This lets you put your hard-earned money into other insurance to cover serious risks that can be financially devastating for your family.

Helping one make correct risk assessment choices is one of the central objectives of this book. "Dying neatly" (and living well until then) requires growing one's ability to distinguish between pains and perils. Pain is discomfort, which can be managed. Peril is serious danger, which can ruin one. Our snow blower example is a pain. A scuffed car bumper or cracked windshield is also a pain. A peril is a whole different degree of experience—it's potentially life changing.

Besides your home, most all catastrophic losses are to your perishable body. Death, disability, and long-term care are the most common risks, but the least dealt with, or communicated about by financial planners. Recall the discussion about insuring a snow blower. Everybody hates being stuck outside in a blizzard with a broken-down snow blower, but as chilling as that situation may be, it's manageable. You can borrow a friend's snow blower. You can get it repaired. You can go back to the trusty old snow shovel. Options abound!

However, your own mortality is much different than a broken snow blower. You can absorb a lot of risk, but premature death is not one of them. If you die, there's no repair shop to fix you up or hardware store to buy another you. You can't borrow "another you" from a friend, and there's no backup of you tucked away in the garage. Therefore, it's critical we do all we can to mitigate the risk

of our deaths because there is no "second chance" for us—
we have to make sure we make the correct choices the
first and only time through life.

Returning to statistics, the picture we're painting is one of
probability versus possibility risk. Low probability events
that would only amount to small losses are not worth insuring (the off chance a kitchen appliance breaks). Likewise, high probability events that would only amount to
small losses are not worth insuring (snow blowers are no-
toriously unreliable, but we can manage).

Then there are high probability events that would be
highly catastrophic. Unfortunately, these types of situa-
tions are almost always impossible or prohibitively expensive to insure. For example, if you build your house a
mile away from an active volcano that's spewing liquid-
hot magma, good luck buying "volcano insurance." A better real-world example is buying hurricane insurance in
southern Florida.

The world I live in is low probability, highly catastrophic
events. Even though there is only a small chance the peri-
lous event may happen, the results would be financially
devastating. I have found that too many people are grossly
underinsured. It could be life insurance, long-term care

insurance, or even disability insurance. We will address each of these specifically later in the book.

I want to focus on life insurance for now. Not only is this my field of expertise, but it is my passion to educate the public about how to protect one's family and legacy from the ultimate financial loss—premature death. People can rebuild their homes and sometimes start new after disability, but death is FINAL.

Decades ago I had an attorney client who paid off his mortgage in his low forties. Since the home was paid off, insurance was no longer mandatory, so he dropped the coverage. As bad luck would have it, his home burned down. Thankfully, nobody was physically hurt, but he did lose irreplaceable items like his family pictures, memorabilia, and medals he earned from the Vietnam War.

As we put together his life insurance and disability insurance policies, he told me in his wise manner, "When my house burned down I thought I lost everything and that my family would never recover. Here we are, five years later, and I have a better house and more assets. I also still have my most valuable asset—my health and ability to earn an income, which would be the biggest loss to my family. I want the maximum insurance to cover this. Everything else is merely *things* and can be replaced."

We all know families who have been devastated by the loss of a young mom or dad. Suppose the surviving parent was in a coma following a fatal car accident and there was no will, no life insurance, no durable power of attorney, and no health care directive. Many problems and questions arise:

1. Who is going to raise the children while the surviving parent is in a coma? Or if both parents die, who will raise the children?

2. Who makes the medical decision to be on life support systems or not?

3. Who signs the legal documents?

4. Who pays for the medical bills?

5. Who provides for the children? Is college an option?

6. How is the remaining family going to maintain their lifestyle?

7. Will charitable donations cease?

8. Where's the money going to come from for all of the above?

A Young Child's Life – A Lesson in "Defensive Financial Planning"

I want you to think about a young child's life. What are the most important elements to a child's healthy development? One of the best diagrams I've seen in my 37 years in the life insurance business is a simple two-by-two square that answers this question by breaking down a child's life into four parts: parent, parent, home, and school. These parts will vary in importance from child to child, but usually these four elements are the most impactful to a child's development.

DIAGRAM: A Child's Ideal Life Elements

Parent 1	**Parent 2**
Home	**School**

Let me explain the diagram. Ideally, every child has two parents to support and love him or her. Although every family is unique and both parents may work in our modern times, often one of the parents focuses more on earning money, freeing the other parent up to have more time to be with the kids and building a home.

The goal of this two-parent arrangement is to enable the child to live in a home that is both developmentally healthy and financially secure. This also allows for the parents to be active in their child's school life, perhaps even opting to send their child to a special school or enroll him or her in unique programs to meet the child's needs.

Suppose we have a family called the Smiths, consisting of two parents and a young son. In this family Parent 1 spends most of the time at home while Parent 2 works outside the house as the sole financial provider. What happens if tragedy strikes and the Parent 2 dies of cancer? The family will be in great financial trouble. Even if we change the scenario and say the parents both earn an equal income, the loss of Parent 2 would mean half their income disappears. It's very likely that this family depends on both incomes to support their lifestyle, so how will this disrupt the son's life?

The most tragic disruption for the Smiths is the loss of the Parent 2, which is hard enough to deal with alone, but the son's upheaval is only beginning. With half the income remaining, life-altering choices will have to be made. Perhaps Parent 1 has to begin working full time or take a second job, but this means the necessary time cannot be invested into building the home like before.

Or perhaps the family must sell their house to downsize or move to a small apartment. Either way, the home element is in disarray, but the school element may also be affected. Perhaps the move results in the son being put in a new school. Maybe he is fortunate to stay at his existing school or at least be geographically close to his existing friends, but perhaps the lack of money means the prior choices of special schools and extra programs are taken away (disrupted).

Let's assume with the Smith's example that Parent 1 has to begin working full time, the house has to be sold, and the son has to be taken out of private school. All four parts of the son's life have been majorly unsettled—no Parent 2 (deceased), less Parent 1 (more time at work), a different home, and an unfamiliar school (including distancing of the son's close friends). See the catastrophic results on the life elements diagram.

DIAGRAM: The Smith Son's Life Elements without Life Insurance

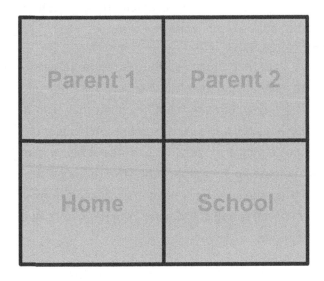

The Smith child's scenario above could have been less severe with proper planning and life insurance. Tragically Parent 2 is gone, but with life insurance the child could have avoided so much unnecessary and agonizing disturbance.

For instance, Parent 1 wouldn't have needed to suddenly leave the home to work full time. Rather, Parent 1 could have taken time off to grieve and be there to support the child emotionally and financially. Plus, the child could have stayed in his or her childhood home and Parent 1 could have even payed off the mortgage. The child also could have stayed in the existing educational structure—the school and programs chosen to most benefit the child.

Take one final look at our diagram to see how much good is done with proper planning to decrease the trauma of a dad's tragic passing. Even though losing a parent is life-altering on everyone involved, instead of possibly 100% of a child's major life elements being thrown in chaos, three of the four elements don't require dramatic disruption.

DIAGRAM: The Smith Son's Life Elements with Life Insurance

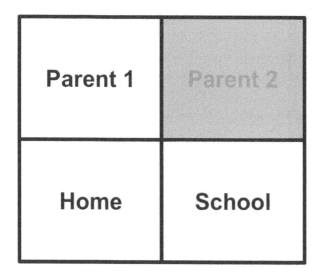

See how the Smiths are able to have blessings even out of tragedy? Parent 1 (and son) will grieve deeply, but will have space to grieve without the burden of earning a paycheck. They both can remain in the same family home (if they desire), while also ensuring the son's school (and schooling options) remain unchanged. This is what "Defensive Financial Planning" is all about—greatly reducing the financial and emotional life disruption of our loved ones.

Now consider something many people say: "I don't need life insurance." Many parents even say this. True, maybe *you personally* don't need it since you'll be dead and gone, but *your family* likely needs it to maintain the lifestyle you desire for them. Imagine if you knew forces were going to attack your family and take your home from you, force your spouse to work, and—if you have kids—damage your children's education. You would absolutely defend against that attack, wouldn't you?

The attack of unexpected death must also be defended against. Your defense starts with understanding a simple truth: **early death can happen to anyone**. Let's consider our philosophy of three possibilities from Chapter 1. We want to hope for the best that our family is never upended by tragedy, yet we must also prepare for the worst. What's worse than your tragic death followed by total disruption of your beloved child's life?

We should *want* to evade such a fate for our families, and Defensive Financial Planning is the *only* way to be prepared! If you think you don't need to worry about death because "that's something that only happens to other people" then you're not defending yourself or your family responsibly! In fact, you're in denial, which just so happens to be the topic of the next chapter.

CHAPTER 4

Denial – Not Just a River in Egypt

My motivation for writing this book lies in my passion to change the perception of death. I want to help people move past denial towards preparation. We simply must "prepare for the worst." Though it is a 100% inevitability, people do not want to talk about death. As to why, there's the obvious reason that the topic is unpleasant. Also, death seems very far off, and there are so many more interesting self-focused topics to pass the time.

Most financial planners are weak in this regard. They are involved merely in the "moving and storage" business of moving money into a better platform and storing it for their clients (hopefully earning a higher yield). While this is important and necessary to accumulate real wealth, there are too many "offensive" financial planners, whom have lost (or were never taught) the art of defensive retirement planning (see Chapter 2). A total comprehensive financial plan has to include both offense and defense. It takes conviction, dedication, and courage to talk about death, disability, and planning for long-term care.

My research, besides 37 years in this great business, comes from interviewing countless people involved in estate planning, including CPAs, CFP®s, attorneys, and others. To get clients to put together an estate plan or purchase "adequate" life insurance boils down to "denial," and this denial means procrastination. "I won't die soon, so I will take care of my estate planning later."

This denial is based on a lack of clear thinking about life expectancy. The truth is each of us has a chance of dying at any age, but statistics tell us the reality is your chance of dying goes up as you age. While denial is the most common feeling, perhaps you've also met someone who is far too high-strung about their death, becoming paranoid. The goal is to neither fall into paranoia or denial but to face reality with a clear mind and peaceful heart. Consider the following diagram:

DIAGRAM: Perception of Life Expectancy

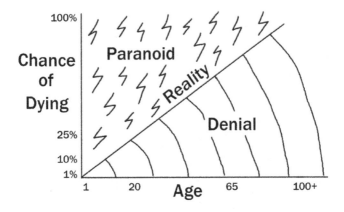

If you want to study life expectancy yourself, you can Google it and find some great calculators. You can input factors like age, weight, height, race, health issues, exercise habits, and so on. I found it very helpful and even though I'm overweight with other factors, I have a 50/50 chance of living to age 90 and a 25% chance of living to age 95. Also see the numbers for a woman aged 60, women aged 40, a man aged 40, and a 30-year-old healthy lean man who works out consistently and doesn't smoke. See the results:[2]

---

[2] Source needed. Include website.

DIAGRAM: Life Expectancy Chances

Gender	Age	Life Expect.	25% Chance	75% Chance	Notes on Health and Lifestyle
Male	65	90	95	82	Overweight, non-smoker, works out 2-3 times a week, no diabetes
Female	60	92	97	84	Overweight, non-smoker, seldom works out, no diabetes
Female	40	97	102	88	Normal weight, non-smoker, works out daily, 1-2 drinks per week, no diabetes
Male	40	74	80	66	Overweight, smoker, rarely works out, 2-7 drinks a week
Male	30	98	104	90	Lean, non-smoker, works out 5-6 times a week, no diabetes

Even if we use generic, non-specific life expectancy numbers provided by the Social Security Administration in 2018, here is what we get:[3]

Age 65 Male   84.2
Age 60 Female 87.1
Age 40 Female 85.5
Age 40 Male   81.6
Age 30 Male   82.1

These numbers are much more general and don't take into consideration health factors and risks, but we can see most people are expected to live into their 80s. However, the real-life expectancy curve is a standard bell curve. There's the average, and then there's a 50/50 chance to be a "die shorter" or "live longer." The following graph

---

[3] Social Security Administration 2020 Longevity Calculations:
https://www.ssa.gov/cgi-bin/longevity.cgi

shows that only 50% of people will be in the "live longer" category. No one likes to admit that they may be a "die shorter" person, but 50% of people will be. This is just math. For everyone who lives beyond age 100, there's someone who will die in the first months of life.

DIAGRAM: Bell Curve for Life Expectancy

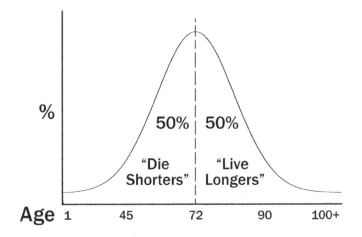

Why is it then that in nearly every seminar or workshop that I do, I give participants some life expectancy numbers and almost everyone raises their hands when I ask, "How many think you will outlive the life expectancy numbers?" Mathematically, it's impossible that 80-90% will outlive the calculations! After almost everyone raises their hands, I say, "Look to your left and then to your right—almost half of you are wrong and will join the "die shorters." God only knows who's who."

One day I'd like to do a seminar where only a quarter of the room raises their hand. Then I could give them the good news that statistically more of them will live longer than they think because ideally in every workshop, assuming equaled balance between healthy and unhealthy people, there would be 50% of the people that raise their hands.

Why are we so optimistic about life expectancy? Why are we in denial about our true possibility of death? What helps me is to play the "what if" game. What if I got into a head-on collision by a drunk driver who swerved over into my lane driving home tonight? Suppose I die instantly, and I'm up in heaven (according to my personal faith beliefs—see Chapter 13) looking down on earth, asking:

1. How does my wife pay the bills?

2. Are the kids still going to college?

3. Can my wife afford the mortgage?

4. Does my wife need to get a better job (or go back to working outside the home)?

5. What if I didn't die instantly but instead went into a coma. Can she legally make decisions on my behalf? Do I have a durable power of attorney?

After I got married, I'd go through this exercise every couple years to make sure I could answer questions about things I'd personally do. For example, here are some steps I've taken:

1. I revised my will to make sure that it includes a health care directive and durable power of attorney and a trust provision for my grandchildren. When my children were younger, Deb and I made provisions for guardianships and trusts for our children should we both die while they were still minors.

2. I purchased a ton of life insurance to pay off our mortgage and other debts. The life insurance proceeds would also let me set aside money in a trust for our children's college. Plus, I'd have enough capital to allow my wife to withdraw 4% cash each year so she would have a comfortable lifestyle and never have to work outside the house (unless she wanted to).

3. I arranged to give 10% of all my assets to charity (as per my faith beliefs).

4. I set up a trust for my grandchildren's (and future great grandchildren's) educational needs.

All this doesn't take much time. It costs a little to setup or change a will and you need to pay those life insurance premiums. I think of premiums as "funding" my "self-completion" clause: I'm ensuring completion of my goals and desires that will happen if I remain alive to see them through. If I don't remain alive, my continued payment of my life insurance premiums until my death is what ensures perfect delivery of what I call it my "last love letter" to my family (see Chapter 6).

The good news is that it doesn't take long and once you do it, you'll have an incredible PEACE OF MIND. Plan for the worst but hope for the best.

Why Most People Won't Do Anything About This "River in Egypt" (Denial)

— Perceptions —

- It's morbid. I don't want to deal with it.

- Not going to happen to me until I'm old

- I'm from a "line of long livers" ("Everyone lives beyond age 90 in my family!")

- I eat right, exercise, and drink safely, so I'm going to live even longer

- America is a "safe" place to live ("It would be different in a third world country")

- The health industry is curing most fatal illnesses and people are living longer

- No one in my family has died young ("So why should I think I'm going to?")

- Too expensive to deal with

- Don't have the time (procrastination)

— Risks —

- What if you're wrong and get cancer or have an accident? Is that worth the risk?

- If the chance is 1% of you dying this year, you say, "no problem..." unless you're the 1%

- The odds are 15-20 times greater of you dying this year than your house burning down!

Are denial and lack of planning worth such catastrophic risks? Let me tell you a very personal story that taught me the harsh reality of loss.

When I was age 21, my brother Mike was 22, and one day he was riding his motorcycle too fast and veered off the road and hit a speed limit sign. Even though he was wearing a helmet, the force of the impact bent the pole, split his helmet, and cracked his forehead. He went unconscious and entered into a coma.

At the time of the accident, I was 1,100 miles away as a sophomore at the U.S. Air Force Academy (USAFA), but when I got the call, I took an emergency flight home the next day to see him. Arriving at the hospital, I saw my poor brother lying there in a coma on life support with his head heavily bandaged. Our family was all there, and my mom was devastated. Her son lay there with no sign of consciousness and there was no way of knowing if he'd ever recover.

Now, let me ask you, do you think my brother Mike woke up? Would it be wise to assume he did? All of us want happy endings, don't we? So it's only natural for people to visit sick loved ones and assume they will "get well" and be okay. Thankfully many people do recover, but to naïvely believe everything will be fine is to dive headlong into denial.

About Mike, I'm going to make you wait in suspense until Chapter 12 (long-term care) to find out his story's conclusion—a conclusion I still think about often to this very day. For now, let me say at age 21, I learned that life is very fragile. We can't count on assumptions and rely on wishes. Likewise, it isn't healthy to fall into negativity and despair.

Therefore, instead of relying on positive-thinking or negative-thinking, clarity comes from reality-based-thinking. To confront the reality of death we must apply the three possibilities from Chapter 1: hope for the best, prepare for the worst, and accept what comes. This is how we get out of denial and live clear-mindedly, which lets us create a plan to "die neatly."

CHAPTER 5

Human Life Value – Your Greatest Financial Asset

"What are you worth on the hoof?" – Marty Polhemus

If you're not a rancher who sells livestock, you may not have ever heard the expression "on the hoof." It's a phrase that specifically applies to how much your livestock is worth before they've been slaughtered. Now maybe this isn't the most delicate way to speak of humans, but have you ever considered what you're worth, financially speaking, while you're currently alive and kicking?

For years I've asked people, "What is your most valuable financial asset?" Inevitably they say, "My home." In this chapter, I want you to realize that your most valuable financial asset is actually *you*. More specifically, it's your expected future earnings, also known as your human life value. Let me explain.

This financial calculation of putting a dollar amount on your life is known as human life value (HLV). Human life value is defined as the present value of expected future earnings of a person. I've been preaching human life value since 1983 and I love to ask young professionals like my niece who just graduated at age 25 from Gonzaga Law School, "What's the largest financial asset that you own?" She rents, has very little furniture, a small savings account, some cash value in a life insurance policy her parents bought, and over $100k in debt (mostly school loans). Her "net worth" is negative on paper.

But that wasn't my question. I asked about her largest financial asset, and the answer is her human life value. At her $65,000/year starting salary if she never got a raise in 40 years it would be $2.6 million in earnings. If during that career she averaged $100k per year, it would be $4 million, and $200k averaged over 40 years would be $8 million! That is her economic potential. That is her human life value.

Two major low probability, high-loss events could devastate her future lifestyle: premature death and disability. Her entire human life value can be lost in the blink of an eye. Like my niece, perhaps you furthered your education to increase your income multiplier for all the years to retirement. This will make you feel better unless you consume it all and don't "plan, protect, and provide" for your family.

I Googled "human life value" to prove my point. Go to a non-insurance company website like LifeHappens.org. You'll find that the average human life value numbers are $3-8 million. So the next time you feel financially depressed think about your HLV as your largest asset. Even if your net worth on paper is depressing, your true financial potential can be inspiring!

A relevant story borne of great tragedy is the findings of the "9/11 Commission." In order to help the survivors of the 9/11/2001 terrorist attacks, the human life value for each of the deceased individuals was calculated using factors such as age and income. The average human life value for 9/11 victims was $1.6 million. (See the table on the next page for the full breakdown).

AGE	$30,000	$50,000	$90,000	$150,000
30	$1,378,746	$1,919,542	$2,938,411	$4,203,648
35	$1,198,974	$1,614,433	$2,398,889	$3,378,319
40	$1,078,306	$1,409,194	$2,035,584	$2,622,558
45	$960,314	$1,212,962	$1,692,085	$2,297,093
50	$859,097	$1,047,634	$1,405,843	$1,859,217
55	$774,251	$909,761	$1,166,885	$1,493,673
60	$700,368	$791,232	$963,643	$1,182,766
65	$650,634	$711,444	$826,829	$973,477

Consider the chart on the next page that lists the estimated human life value of people at various ages who earn between $50k and $200k a year.

DIAGRAM: Human Life Value (Earnings to Age 65)

Age/ Income	$50k	$100k	$150k	$200k
25	$2M	$4M	$6M	$8M
35	$1.5M	$3M	$4.5M	$6M
45	$1M	$2M	$3M	$4M
55	$500k	$1M	$1.5M	$2M

When I was trained in this business, I was taught that there are only three things that can happen to you: you live, you die, or you become disabled. In human life value terms, you either will reach the full potential (you live), you lose it all (you die), or it's greatly diminished (you become disabled). In light of these scenarios, three questions arise:

1. How much of your human life value are you going to protect? Against...

   a. disabling injury

   b. premature death

2. Is your level of protection enough to insure the lifestyle for you and your loved ones?

3. How much are you going to save or invest to replace your income later?

Businesses compute human life value for their "key employees." Suppose the sales manager is responsible for over $2 million per year in sales and is killed in an auto accident. How much revenue is lost? How is the business going to replace him/her?

Businesses need to quantify the value of their key people and decide if they want to insure against that loss. This is called "Key Person Life Insurance." I sincerely believe in this and have sold hundreds of these policies.

"Take away my buildings, my equipment, and all of my inventory, and give me back my people. I will have it all back in 3-5 years." – Andrew Carnegie, Steel Baron in the Early 1900s

One of my mentors, Marty Polhemus (more on Marty later), was an HLV guru. He instilled in me the following three powerful HLV stories: Cash Suitcase Buyout, The

Money Machine, and Attorney from Ohio. I share these stories in order to increase belief in the amount of life insurance to own.

Story One – Cash Suitcase Buyout

Imagine me doing an initial consultation with a young professional woman (age 30-45) with a family. I ask, "How much life insurance do you own?" I get her answer of $500k. She's a pharmacist making $170k/year with two kids and a homemaking husband. So I ask, "How do you feel about the amount of life insurance you currently own?" She then will either say "good" or "bad."

If she says, "Bad," she's ready to buy more life insurance. If she says, "Good," I have a problem. I think she's grossly underinsured, and she thinks she has enough. Most agents wimp out here and figure some life insurance is "better than none." Or they go with the "sell them what they want" excuse, but most people don't know how to equate the death benefit amount of their life insurance to the future lifestyle they want for their families.

In order to open the understanding of the prospective client, what I do is "buy out their income," by taking their life insurance amount, income, and years to age 65. This procedure can be illustrated with the following story:

Suppose I have a suitcase filled with $500,000 cash (the amount of life insurance on the primary wage earner). Thousand-dollar bills all bundled up like in a mob movie. I slide the suitcase across the table and offer to buy out their future income with the money in the suitcase.

"I'll give you this suitcase, but you still have to work 40/50hrs per week from now until age 65, and all of the money you earn will be automatically deposited into my checking account. Are we "in or out?" They usually say, "no way." So I keep upping—perhaps doubling—the amount until they give in.

> *Me: "How about $1 million?"*
>
> *Client: "No way."*
>
> *Me: "$2 million?"*
>
> *Client: "Still not close."*
>
> *Me: "$4 million? Before you say, "no," have you heard of the 4% rule?*
>
> *Client: "No, what's that?"*
>
> *Me: "Basically, you should be able to invest money in a conservative portfolio and withdraw 4% per year and still preserve the principal. With that in mind, $4 million at 4% is $160,000 per year perpetually. So is $4 million your number?"*
>
> *Client: "How about $6 million?"*

Me: "That's a good number. At 4% that would be $240,000 per year, which is more than you're currently earning per year, but it might be a good estimate of your average income from now until age 65. So is that your number?"

Client: "Yes."

Me: Thinking, "Ah, we've finally reached a number you feel good about." [With our mutually agreed upon number, I can now continue our discussion.]

Me: "So I'm confused. You're telling me that you won't sell me your future income for less than $6 million, but you're going to give your beautiful family only $500k if you die [use your hands and have one high for the $6 million and one low for the $500k]. Can't we compromise somewhere in the middle?"

Now I'm ready to try to get the client to agree to some middle-range number and stick with it. I keep urging the client to understand that they already know their life is worth much more than their current life insurance value. Once the client awakens to this truth, he or she will realize that he or she is grossly underinsured and will hopefully buy more.

For the record, I've used this "Cash Suitcase" story successfully many times. My favorite story involves a doctor client. Another agent asked me to go to lunch with a doctor making $400,000 per year. The doctor also brought his wife along with him. I began the conversation by asking him how much life insurance he currently owned. He said $1 million. Then I asked him how he felt about this amount. He responded with "good."

I knew he was grossly underinsured because of human life value math based on a $400,000/year income. So I proceeded to guide him through the "Cash Suitcase" illustration. When it came time for him to put a price on his future earnings, his wife helpfully chimed in and said I'd have to give them a cool $10 million. Thanks to her astute calculation, I turned to the doctor and said that $10 million was a good number because at 4% that would replace his $400,000/year income. Then I asked if he was "okay" with his wife only getting $1 million if he died. The next week he bought another $5 million, and I (and likely his wife!) felt a lot better about his coverage! This is the power of understanding human life value through clear illustrations.

By the way, when clients with existing life insurance policies buy from me, I usually keep their existing life insurance because I don't want to "replace." I want to build a "life insurance portfolio" (see Chapter 7), which usually involves multiple policies.

I have never had a client die with too much life insurance. I have, however, had a number of "wimpy" payouts, and each one made me regret not being a better agent for the sake of the families. Protect your human life value robustly enough to keep your family in the lifestyle you promised them.

Story Two – The Money Machine

With this story you have to be a little bit of an artist. Draw the "money machine" below and have the money coming out per month based on your client's income (minimum $5,000/month).

DIAGRAM: Money Machine

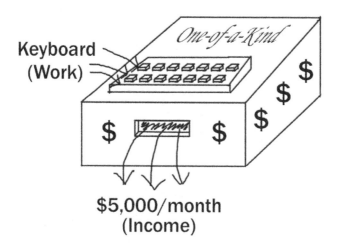

Keyboard (Work)

One-of-a-Kind

$5,000/month
(Income)

After drawing the previous picture, I begin the following discussion.

Me: "Suppose you have a MONEY MACHINE. It was issued to you when you turned 25 and every 1ˢᵗ of the month it spits out $5,000—fifty Ben Franklins! All you do is plug in the security code and your fingerprint and voìla—the money flow happens.

Well, the problem is that there are no replaceable parts in this particular money machine, and you can only get one in a lifetime. But, my company, "Money Machine, Inc," can insure your machine for any amount you want. Do you want to insure it?"

Client: "Absolutely."

Me: "For how many years?"

Client: "For the rest of my life!"

Me: "So $5,000/month is $60,000/year. For 60 years that's $3.6 million, so that's the amount we should insure it for, right?"

Client: "Yes."

Me: "Well, I have some good news. If we only insure it for $1.5 million and you invest it properly, you should be able to withdraw 4% per year— $60,000/year—and keep the principal. It's a perpetual money machine. Does that make sense?"
[The "4% rule" says that properly invested money

should earn at least 4% a year, meaning you can withdraw 4% each year without reducing your investment principal.]

Client: "Yes."

Me: "Well, I'm sure that you're a great father, super husband and friend, but, economically, you're a 'money machine.' You go to work, bring home cash day after day, but one day the bus hits you and no more income. I want to replace your future income with the right amount of protection."

Again, remember with the 4% rule, $1 million is just $40k/year. Most people should own $2 million to $10 million of life insurance. They don't because as an industry we have wimped out communicating human life value!

Story Three –Attorney from Ohio

Me: "So, let's pretend I knock on your door and say, 'My name is [Jim Lusk]. I'm an attorney from Ohio, and I need to verify your identity. Is this [client's name] with Social Security Number [make up 9 digits]? [Play along and say, 'Yes.']

You just inherited a $300,000 apartment complex from your great aunt that is fully rented and pays the owner $40,000 per year after paying the manager and expenses. I need to know the answer to two questions."

Me: "Question number one: Do you want the property?"

Client: "Yes!"

Me: [I pretend to have them sign a contract to take ownership.] "Our law firm agrees that this would be a good decision."

Me: "Question number two: Do you want to continue the fire insurance on the building? You see, when your great aunt died, the insurance was in her name, so the fire insurance lapsed. The premium would be $2,000/year. We don't think you should insure it because you'd only get $38k a year instead of the full $40k.

I have a form here to sign that says you don't want the insurance." [I pretend to put another contract in front of the client and look at their face.]

Client: "No way! I want to insure it!"

Me: "Why?"

Client: "I still get $38k/year!"

Me: "Yes, but you didn't even have it 2 minutes ago."

Client: "Well, I do now, and I don't want to lose it. So insure it!"

Me: "So, you think it's that important to insure future income?"

Client: "Yes."

Me: "Which is more likely to occur: this apartment building burning down or you dying?"

Client: "I don't know."

Me: "Statistics tell us there's about a 15-20 times greater chance of dying within a year for a male, age 22, than for a house burning down. Which one do you think would be more catastrophic to your family: this apartment complex burning down or you dying?"

Client: "Me dying."

Me: "So, you'll spend $2,000 a year to insure a $38,000 cash flow, but you won't spend that amount to insure your own life for $3,000,000?"
Client: "I get it. Let's buy the life insurance."

Conclusion to the Three Stories

Throughout my years I've used all three of these human life value stories numerous times, especially "The Money Machine." Once people realize their lives (in human life value terms) are a one-of-a-kind device for achieving their financial dreams, they see the wisdom in insuring their own futures through life insurance.

I use the "Cash Suitcase Buyout" story anytime someone has an inadequate amount of life insurance and feels good about it. I need to help you feel the weakness of your current position or you won't change your philosophy.

The "Attorney from Ohio" story is yet another descriptive method of enlightening people to the great financial value they've been gifted within themselves. From this position of positivity, people can see how life insurance protects their future income.

I was told as a young life insurance agent that "if you're accused of being a life insurance agent, make sure that there's enough evidence to convict you." I'm totally convinced that if your life insurance agent doesn't include HLV calculations that deal with income replacement of "money machines" (your HLV), find one who does.

For you professionals out there who have spent maybe hundreds of thousands of dollars for advanced degrees and education so you can make a lot more money (doctors, dentists, attorneys, etc.), the loss of income can be enormous because you have become phenomenal *money machines*. Your family's lifestyle is likely much greater than the average family. That's wonderful and congratulations, but you also have a lot more to lose if the money machine shuts down (death) or starts to sputter (disability).

For the rest of you who aren't on the extreme end of money machine performance, it's still immensely important to protect yourself because your financial potential is by far your most valuable financial asset. Protect the loss of your human life value with millions of dollars of life insurance, and then make sure you also protect against being disabled (see Chapter 11).

I know the two catastrophic events of death and disability are hard to deal with, but the reality is that a good "defense plan" has to properly insure your loss of income. You simply cannot "die neatly" without properly understanding your human life value. So understand your financial potential and take the next step of buying the right amount of life insurance your family needs, which leads into the next chapter.

CHAPTER 6

Life Insurance – Your Last Love Letter

With our spouses, many of us have written love letters to each other over the years (and hopefully we still write such letters). We write these letters to express our love, appreciation, and respect for the other person, and it's amazing how many my wife has saved. What makes a love letter important is being written from the heart's true desire. As strange as it may sound, this same passion is why I own so much life insurance—because I desire my family members to live out their lives as best as possible. Maybe you've never connected life insurance with love letters, but allow me to explain.

When people find out I own a large sum of life insurance, they almost always ask me the same question: "Why?" It's not because I'm rich (I wouldn't consider myself wealthy). It's because I love my family! Out of this love, I've made my wife Debbie and my family a lot of promises about taking care of their needs, and if I'm blessed to live long enough, I believe these promises will be fulfilled.

However, what if I die prematurely? I won't be around to work on my promises (or write any more literal love letters), but I still want the "lifestyle promises" to come to fruition for my family. This is why I've made sure to prepare one final "love letter" that is sealed until the time of my death. This letter contains not empty hopes, but assurances that my love will continue beyond my death through the "miracle" of life insurance, which gives blessings to others in the future and "peace of mind" to me in the present.

This letter contains the following guarantees: the mortgage can be paid off, credit cards and other debts can be paid off, other final expenses like funeral costs and medical bills can be paid off, a trust can be established for the grandchildren to pay for college or trade school, and significant sums can be donated to worthy charities (see Chapter 10).

Most importantly, my wife will have enough monthly income to last the rest of her life without having to work outside the home. Even accounting for inflation, she'll be able to have the "same lifestyle" she's accustomed to. Isn't that what love is? To look beyond ourselves—our own lives—and prepare to bless those that we love even through our own passing into the afterlife.

So how do I ensure I can deliver on my promises? The only way is by having enough capital (money) "created" upon death to replace my lost income. I call life insurance a "miracle" because it arrives at the perfect time, just when it's needed the most (when Chapter 5's "money machine" is put out of commission).

Life insurance is one of the few financial contracts that matures upon an event rather than time. If we have enough time, we can make more money. But what if time runs short and I haven't accumulated enough money? Then what? What you've earned for your family when you die is what you have. Nothing more can be earned, but life insurance goes beyond death and transforms your lost time into money for your family. Consider the following illustration:

Imagine building a house for your family. You've got the foundation up and maybe some of the walls, but then a "forever winter" hits and you're never able to work on the house again. This "forever winter" is what happens with premature death.

However, assume at the very moment this "forever winter" hits, a wholly built and ready-to-use house is provided to your family, welcoming them into warmth and safety. This salvation from the cold would feel like a miracle to most, but this is what life insurance provides.

We're each building a financial house for our families, which takes so many decades to "complete" as we build our careers, establish investment and retirement accounts, and hopefully reach the end stages of abundance to pass on to future generations. But if we die in the middle of those decades of work, our financial house remains incomplete, our personal financial capability (Chapter 5's "human life value") is "frozen" by the "forever winter" of death.

However, if we have life insurance, our policy steps in to miraculously "thaw" the "forever winter" and provide our family that warm and safe financial building that we would have completed in our remaining decades of life, had we the chance. So life insurance (with a trusted agent and company) acts like a backup team of builders that comes in when needed to give your family what you tragically can no longer provide.

I am sure almost everyone reading this loves his or her family, but if you tragically pass away, your family needs to know their financial house won't collapse but will be built even without you. This is why I call life insurance your "last love letter." So, let me ask you, do you have a good "last love letter" proving your devotion to your family, even in their life after your death?

It's been often asked about life insurance why it's not called death insurance because you have to die to collect it. The answer is easy: life insurance is for the *life* of the survivors. You're ensuring your family gets the *life* you want for them when you pass. The bottom line is that if you want your family to have a guaranteed lifestyle should you die prematurely, there are only a few options.

1. Be extremely wealthy. Good luck.

2. Win the lottery. Even luckier!

3. Count on rich relatives to take care of your family. We're getting very risky now.

4. Own a great life insurance portfolio (usually more than one policy) that's large enough to pay off debts and replace lost income.

I don't personally have any of the first three options, and I don't recommend you rely on them either. Most people sadly "default" to drastically reducing their family's lifestyle, but you can avoid this by going with our fourth option: a great life insurance portfolio.

I have opted for this option because it's the only one I can guarantee after my death. So I have chosen to create a great life insurance plan and reviewed it with my wife because I want her to know my love for her is still strong. Even if this "last love letter" isn't quite as flowery as the ones when we first met, I bet she'll remember it much longer as she lives out her years with financial freedom. Plus, I'll bet she'll be very glad I loved her enough to "sacrifice the premiums today for a better tomorrow."

But life insurance doesn't just benefit us in the future. My wife already receives wonderful "peace of mind," which is very important to her, knowing that upon my death she will not have financial burdens. She won't have to get an unfulfilling job or quickly marry some "rich guy" to support her. Naturally, my wife would rather have me live a long fruitful life with her, but she agrees this is the best "last love letter" I could give her.

For these reasons, I call life insurance "your last love letter." What do you want your family to know after you're gone? I want them to know they're still going to be taken care of because I still love them, even after death. Plus, it feels so good to know I've planned for my family's future—that I've taken steps to "die neatly." This is the "miracle" of life insurance.

CHAPTER 7

Life Insurance 101 – The Basics

Despite my high praises of life insurance, in today's world it can be such a controversial, misused, and mistrusted term that conjures up visions of obnoxious salespeople and intimidating legal gibberish. The result is that many people have almost entirely given up looking into the concept. Think about it! When was the last time you and/or your significant other woke up on a day off and said, "Hey honey, let's go shopping for some life insurance?"

However, as discussed last chapter, life insurance is truly a *powerful* way to express your love. Think about it this way: Hardly anyone who buys life insurance buys it for their own selfish reasons. It's only something you buy if you're serious about caring for others in your life. So why don't more people buy life insurance? I think so much of it has to do with the confusion as much as denial (as discussed in Chapter 4), and we tend to fear what we don't understand.

Therefore, I doubt anyone has ever woken up all excited to go life insurance shopping, but even people who recognize the need for life insurance can so easily get stuck. For years I've had potential clients say, "This looks good, but I need to shop and compare." Really? I don't think they did anything afterward. They just went back to swimming in that "River in Egypt" because it's familiar and seems safe enough.

The purpose of this chapter is to help give you the courage and knowledge to take the next step in beginning to write "your last love letter," as daunting as the task may seem. With technology today you can easily find answers to this shopping dilemma. I would start with LifeHappens.org (they even have an HLV calculator). This resource is not funded by one insurance company, it was started by NAIFA.

In fact, one of the criteria I'd use to choose an insurance adviser is if they are a member of NAIFA. If not, why not? I love NAIFA so much that I'm donating part of the sale of each book to them as my way of giving back (see Chapter 10) for all they've done for me and many others to grow and serve in the life insurance business.

Another resource is to Google your life insurance questions. When you do that, sort out the answers that are biased by only one company. Try to stick with 3rd party research. The Life Insurance and Market Research Association[4] (LIMRA) is a great reference.

AMBest is the authority for rating life insurance companies, but one problem is the highest rating (A++) is only available if the company is massive. There are many A and A+ carriers that are great companies to buy from. My recommendation is to make sure you purchase a product (contract) from an old (greater than 120 years old) highly rated "A" or better company.

Understanding this confusing industry takes a lot of time, so it's important to have a quality experienced agent whom you can trust. If you're working with a newer agent, ask who their mentor was and grade the mentor for experience and credentials (e.g. the initials after their name, most importantly CLU®, ChFC®, and CFP®). Otherwise, it could be "the blind leading the blind."

So, you have a good agent and a good company. Now what? Let's learn about the different types of insurance to help you confirm or negotiate with your agent. You can also use this information to respectfully challenge your

---

[4] The Life Insurance and Market Research Association.
https://www.limra.com/en/

agent to determine his or her biases. Now let me explain the basics of life insurance.

Life Insurance 101

Fundamentally, there are only two types of life insurance: term and permanent. There is a place for both kinds, so here I disagree with people who make definitive statements like "term insurance is the only way to go." Two comments follow.

First, my mother used to say, "always and never are two words you should always remember and never use." Any time someone takes an absolute "this way or the highway" attitude, the first thing I do is look for an exception. I love the answer that attorneys give to most questions: "it depends."

Second, people who claim there is only *one way* to get life insurance usually aren't qualified to make such statements. If someone is taking a hardline approach with you, you would be very wise to ask for that person's credentials. Most likely, they don't have proper credentials, which is why they must make strong sounding statements as a way to hide their own confusion on the complexities of life insurance.

So when my clients ask, "should I buy term insurance or permanent?" I like to say, "It depends on how long you want the life insurance." Most of my clients have both. I recommend when you're younger (and hopefully very healthy) to buy millions of dollars of inexpensive term life insurance. Use the term for the short duration. As you build your "financial house" you can drop some of it (stop paying) or possibly convert it to permanent life insurance. Once older and can afford it, buy permanent for the only policies that you can't outlive (and want to keep until age 100+ for example).

Here are some main differences between term and permanent life insurance:

Term Life Insurance

- Like renting—cheaper earlier in your life

- Increasing premium at some time

- No equity—no cash value

- Pays "if you die" during the term

- Self-evicting: the company has designed the product to "evict you" before life expectancy

- Cheaper (lower cost) early then reality hits—it gets more expensive as you get older

- 20- & 30-year term is just "prefunding" future mortality charges—like prepaying rent. That would be ok, but over 75% are lapsed or replaced within 10 years. So you "prepaid" and never received a discount later.

- Death benefit only: No living benefits (like most insurance policies, home, auto, etc.)

- Possible payout (only on about 1% of all policies)

Permanent Life Insurance

- Like owning—higher premium, but some goes into equity

- Level premium—can be guaranteed to never increase

- For life if funded properly, even beyond age 100

- Equity (called cash value) is accessible "tax-free" if set up properly

- Pays "when you die" (versus "if" with term insurance)

- Self-completing: you don't have to pay for life to get lifetime coverage

- More expensive earlier, but level offset by cash value

- Inevitable Death benefit plus access to "living benefit" (cash value)—for "pennies on the dollar"

- Can provide accelerated money for long-term care, terminal illness, or other critical illness

DIAGRAM: Life Insurance – Term versus Permanent (Curved Line vs Flat Line)

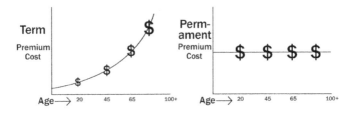

I had a 60-year-old client who was one year into a 20-year term policy that he thought was going to pay for his future estate taxes. I called the company, talked to an actuary, and at a "preferred" rate there was a 91% chance that he would outlive the policy (19 years later). Why would anyone buy term insurance for the inevitable estate taxes due upon death? Consider the adage "you can't solve a permanent problem with a temporary solution." At year 21, the policy's premiums skyrocketed exponentially.

On the other hand, I have a business client who has a $5 million, 10-year loan from a bank, and the bank insisted on covering the loan with the "assignment" of a life insurance policy. This is a perfect 10-year term policy, although I still recommend "convertible" term with a highly rated company. That way if his health went bad and he becomes uninsurable, he or she would have the ability to convert or change to a permanent policy without having to requalify health-wise.

This brings up my philosophy of term insurance. When my clients insist on term insurance, I ask them if they want "cheap term" or "good term." "Cheap term" you can buy on the internet or some 1-800 number. You don't need an agent and you are convinced that the lowest cost is always better. This faulty philosophy can stick you with a low rated company and no conversion privileges (see below). It's like my mother used to say, "Cheap things aren't good and good things aren't cheap."

With that in mind, for years I've preached and taught that "good term" might be a little higher premium, but it's with a "highly rated" company and is "convertible." Convertible is like a "lease with option to buy" without having to requalify physically or otherwise. Another saying is "if you're going to rent, rent in the right neighborhood." This means going with the right company that you want a lifelong contract with.

Many people listen to the "term only" philosophy that says you should never buy permanent life insurance because you should "buy term insurance and invest the difference." This means you set aside the money you *would have* paid on the more expensive permanent life insurance premiums and invest it yourself, say, in mutual funds. Here are some problems with this logic:

1. It takes much financial effort and self-control to "buy term insurance and invest the difference." In my experience, most people just aren't disciplined or organized enough to save money on a consistent basis when there isn't a structure in place that facilitates wise financial behaviors. Rather than invest the difference for the future, most people fall into the rut of enjoying the difference now. So, why not let permanent life insurance be the structure to guide wise financial planning? Whether it's whole life, variable universal life, or index universal life (the most popular today), well-planned policies let you enjoy a 4-6% rate of return over 20 years, rather than consuming the savings in the present.

2. Term insurance eventually runs out and since only about 1% pays a claim, are you sure you want to lose that coverage? The saying is "buy term and invest the difference because you don't need life insurance at age 65." I've been in the life insurance business for over 37 years and I've never met a 65-year-old who didn't want life insurance— rather they just don't want to pay those "high" premiums.

My goal today is to design life insurance portfolios for young families that have the following:

1. **No more premiums at age 65-67.** The policies are either "self-paying" via earnings or the term insurance remaining is dropped.

2. **Lifetime protection.** We "fund" the death benefits to at least age 100. The death benefit is probably less than when they had kids, but people love this inevitable payday.

3. **Tax-free access to the cash value.** If policies are designed properly and funded correctly, there is "tax-free" access based on today's tax laws.

That can't be accomplished with term insurance. Remember, you can't solve a permanent problem with a "temporary solution." Below are two problems that need a "permanent solution"—therefore term insurance doesn't work.

1. **Estate tax liquidity.** Many large (multimillion dollar) policies today are owed by trusts to pay for future estate taxes upon the death of wealthy people. The policies must be in force at death or the plan fails. If the client dies at age 90, for example, no term insurance is left. But, if it's funded with permanent life insurance there will be an inevitable payout for pennies on the dollar.

2. **Pension option planning.** I have written an entire booklet (Retirement Pension Options) that is available for order on my website (www.retirementnationwide.com). Basically, if you have a pension with income options for a surviving spouse (called a "defined benefit pension"—see the next chapter), it's reduced from a "single life" annuity payout. What this means is the reduction is actually a premium for life insurance. So why not buy directly from a life insurance company (if you qualify) and do better? Term insurance doesn't work for this pension option planning.

The Life Insurance Portfolio

There is no "end-all, catch-all" policy for everyone because life changes, needs change, income changes, and hopefully you retire one day. Do you want life insurance after retirement? People do, they just don't want the expensive premiums!

What I've taught for years is first decide what is the "right" amount of coverage (whether a mix of term or permanent) through a cash/income analysis (as discussed in Chapter 5 "Human Life Value"). Buy more not less if you're young (term insurance is really low-cost when you're young).

Secondly, have as much permanent life insurance in either index universal life or whole life ("participating" or "mutual") and put 5-7% of your gross income into these types of accumulation tools for college savings, mortgage pay off, business opportunities, and tax-free income at retirement (like ROTH IRAs). David McKnight, in his book, "The Power of Zero,"[5] has a chapter entitled "LIRP" (Life Insurance Retirement Plan) that is the best explanation of this policy.

So the graph looks like the one below. You commit a budget for this portfolio and increase allocations, or convert more term life insurance to permanent later with a stroke of a pen. "X" is the amount of permanent life insurance and "Y" is the total death benefit.

---

[5] The Power of Zero. David McKnight. Acanthus Publishing. 2014.

DIAGRAM: Life Insurance Portfolio

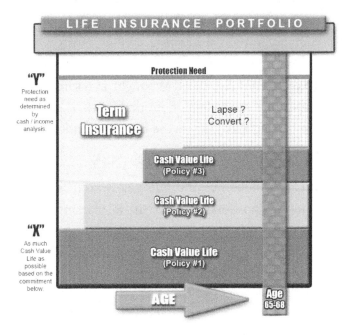

Concluding Life Insurance 101

A mix of wisely chosen term and permanent life insurance is needed to balance out a complete life insurance portfolio. Part of the wisdom comes from identifying related pitfalls from other investments, which leads us into what I call the worst life insurance policy ever.

CHAPTER 8

Spousal Reduced Pension – The Worst Life Insurance Policy Ever (Unless You Have Insurability Issues)

This chapter is about one of my biggest passions: optimizing pension payouts. I want clients who participate in defined benefit pensions to get the most money they are entitled to, and this means navigating the complicated world of spousal survivor benefits. Broadly speaking, a person has two choices: receive the full amount for yourself but nothing for your spouse or take a reduced benefit amount but have payments continue to your spouse if you die first.

How do you decide what is best? It starts with realizing that when you opt for survivor benefits for your spouse, you are, in fact, buying a life insurance policy from your pension, and the premium is, in fact, the amount your pension is reduced by. With this background, let me present you with a life insurance offer and see what you think. Here are some facts about the policy:

1. You will pay your entire life with premiums increasing at 2-3% per year.

2. The death benefit is a taxable monthly income for your spouse.

3. There's also no lump sum tax-free benefit or accelerated benefit for terminal illness.

4. There's no equity or cash value while you're alive (money disappears like term insurance).

5. Your spouse is the only beneficiary, and if he or she dies first you will still pay premiums (unless your pension has a "pop-up" clause), and no one gets the survivor benefit.

6. If you both die, your children or estate lose any "contingent beneficiary" payout.

7. You pay the same premium as a 65-year-old smoker with emphysema.

Would you purchase this policy?

I have been in the business since 1983. Prior to this, I taught high school math and physics, and I understood my pension at age 22. I also knew that if I wanted my wife to have a survivor benefit, I had to take about a 20% reduction in my pension in order to do that. If I died, the monthly income would continue to her. I looked at that and said, "That's a lot of money!" Plus, I realized I had to give up a lot of flexibility and control. Let me assure you, it is a lot of money, and people do give up a lot of flexibility and control. They pick a survivor benefit for their spouse (a lifetime decision) with only some 30 seconds of thought.

The problem is over 80% of married retirees with defined benefit pensions take reduced survivor options for their spouses. The reduced survivor option is in fact just what I outlined above as the "worst life insurance policy ever." Remember, if you take any reduced pension because you "love your spouse," you are simply buying a life insurance policy from your pension where the death benefit is a non-transferable lifetime annuity for your spouse only.

What I've done for 37 years is to help people understand this policy and see if there's a better policy in the private sector whereby they can take the difference—what we'll call "the spread"—and use that for a premium for your own personal life insurance. We want this life insurance to be large enough to give your spouse a survivor benefit equal to what the pension would have provided.

This strategy of covering "the spread" on your spousal versus non-spousal coverage of your defined benefit pension plan with life insurance makes so much sense to most people that I often am asked, "Why doesn't everybody do this?" I respond by saying there are two reasons why people don't do this. First, they don't know about it. Second, they don't qualify. Let's discuss both.

1. They don't know about it. It's fascinating how many people in my 37 years in the business simply don't know about, or have never considered, this covering strategy. My mentor, Virginia Faust, was the director of the Washington State Teacher's Retirement System and said, "It's amazing that people spend a month to plan a week's vacation in Hawaii, and yet they'll work for 30 years but won't take an hour or two to plan the rest of their life."

I believe that people who work for the State (or other public agencies) often simply assume "the State will take care of me." They've been lulled into a warm feeling that their great pension is all they need. When they get the options from the pension office, the office tells them to pick one of three or four options, but most people aren't prepared to make such critical decisions on the fly. So in that moment, they base which box to check on a few tidbits of knowledge. Knowing they need to get the forms done, they just "check the box" and move on with their lives. That 30-second ill-informed irrevocable decision is how many pension-covered people "plan" their retirement for years to come.

Therefore, they don't know about other options. Almost *no* government pension administrator or office worker is going to sit them down and inform them of more beneficial and wise retirement strategies, because those other workers probably don't know about these other options either! Also, the workers are usually advised to not recommend one option or the other because the company/pension could be liable if things don't go well for the retiree.

Given the missing personal knowledge, rush to get the paperwork done, and the lack of guidance from the plan administrators, countless people make serious financial choices without investigating or going shopping to see what's available. It's a sad situation because we're talking about one of the largest financial decisions that you will ever make if you have a defined benefit pension. Take some time, do some research and find out more about it. A great place to go is to my website: www.retirementnationwide.com and get a free booklet ("Retirement Pension Options") on how to set up this pension option plan I'm describing.

2. They don't qualify. If you're going to go into the private insurance market, you have to qualify for it physically. A lot of people think they won't qualify because they have high blood pressure or marginal cholesterol levels. We can still get good ratings with those minor things. However, it's hard to qualify for it if you are a cancer survivor within the last three or four years or if you have a heart condition or diabetes. These are the big ones that really hit you hard on the premiums.

In the worst case, you could be uninsurable altogether. Therefore, it may be in your best interest to simply take the "ugly" policy because that's the only thing available to you. The point of sharing the reality of high premiums or uninsurability isn't to scare you, though. The point is, regardless of your health, you won't know what the rates are until you go shopping and see what rates are for you. (Even if you don't qualify, the survivor benefit options are guaranteed, regardless of your health, age, race, etc.) The other point is that the younger you are, the lower the premium, and better health lets you lock in your insurability.

So now, how do you find a better life insurance policy? I highly recommend that, first of all, you find a good agent who specializes in pension option planning. Pension option planning is designed to solve the question: "how do you get the most income from your pension and still have an insurance policy that's large enough to give a survivor benefit equal to what the state would provide?" It's not easy. Most agents don't know how to calculate that death benefit or which policy is the best for the client. Likewise, many financial planners are oblivious to this problem and won't integrate a solution into your financial plan.

Secondly, make sure whatever agent you pick has access to more than one company so they can shop the market for you. Also make sure your agent chooses highly rated companies over 120 years old, which proves they have a track record through the Great Depression, major wars, and so on.

Too many people take this reduced pension that they cannot change after they elect, and then live a long time. Longevity is one of the biggest factors. By living a long time they give up hundreds of thousands of dollars in order to give a survivor benefit to their spouse, and the longer you live, the higher the chance that your spouse will have health concerns and maybe even be in a nursing home without receiving benefits. It's highly possible that you could give up all this money through the years and then your spouse, upon your death, may *never* recoup the amount of money you gave up to provide them the spouse benefit in the first place. That's a sad situation.

On the other hand, what if you both die at the same time? God forbid you're together in your motorhome driving across the country and a drunk driver swerves into you and you both pass away. How much of your pension money continues to your kids or estate? If you rely on your pension's survivor benefit, *nothing* goes to them. However, if we do a private insurance policy of, say, $1 million, that $1 million is income *tax-free* to your estate.

That could be a big difference in your children's or other family members' lives!

These policies also have extra benefits, including when you pay money into them there's equity or cash value that you can access tax-free (if set up correctly). This money could be accessed for any reason without penalty. For instance, if you needed money to pay for the deductible on a medical insurance policy or if your children wanted to borrow money to buy a house, this policy allows you to access its cash value. You can pay it back when you want, or it could be paid back upon death. The policy administrators look at how much money you've taken out over the years. Most other financial vehicles do not have this "any reason cash" option. Again, if you took the reduced pension, there is *no* equity, *no* cash value, and *no* account or living benefits to access and no guaranteed pay out.

The other living benefits that can be available are part of the $1 million for long-term care needs (chronic care), critical illnesses, or terminal illnesses. Good policies have a way to access some of this money if you cannot do two of the six activities of daily living or have significant "cognitive impairment" (see Chapter 11 on long-term care). You could advance the monies ahead of time tax-free before you died. These "hybrid" policies are available in today's market and do an incredible job of providing flexibility.

The last thing is, if your spouse pre-deceases you, then what are your options? One option is you could just surrender this policy and get some money back. Another option is you could keep the policy and it would pay to your children or your estate upon your death. If you don't like the premiums for this policy, you could actually let the kids pay the premiums for you, and they would receive the inevitable payout upon your death of the $1 million. There are a lot of options and flexibility that can be decided 20-30 years later in many cases once insurability is set. The key principle is that by taking the reduced spousal pension option, you give up a ton of flexibility, too much money, and an estate value for your children/heirs.

The last part of this discussion has to do with the question, "When do you buy this life insurance policy?" It's a fascinating question. A lot of people tell me, "Well, I'm going to wait until the day I retire, and then I will buy the life insurance from you. I know I'll be 62 years old [if they take early retirement], but I really don't want to spend any money on life insurance until that point." Now, let's suppose this person is 50 years old when he or she has this discussion with me. I have five priorities in my conversation.

Priority #1: Premium Difference. My first priority is to talk about the difference in premiums between an age 50-year-old and an age 62-year-old. I show them this difference—premiums at age 50 being less than *half* that of age 62!—and explain that assuming they live to age 90 the person who started at 50 would actually pay less total premiums than the person who started at age 62. The numbers are fascinating—study the math yourself!

Priority #2: Changing Health. The second priority is to determine if the 50-year-old is healthy. Let's assume they're a non-smoker with no medications. What's the chance by age 62 that they still will have no medication and be in that same state of good health? The nice thing about buying insurance early is that you are almost always healthier than you are going to be in the future. So I talk to my clients about "freezing your health" and locking in the coverage that the life insurance company can never change.

A life insurance policy is really just a unilateral (one-sided) contract with a big insurance company. They can never change your rating and have to fulfill their promises. You, on the other hand, are not bound to anything but paying premiums. You can fall ill, go through hard times, and even get out of the contract later.

Priority #3: Start Sooner. The third priority is to start earlier rather than later. Let's say that you buy a policy that you only pay premiums on for 20 years. If you start at 50, you're done at 70. If you wait until 62, you're done at age 82. The sooner you start, the sooner you're done, and the sooner you start, the less total premium cost to you!

Priority #4: Pre-Retirement Payments. The number four priority is to consider which of the following is easier to pay: when you're still working at your current position or after you've retired and likely taken a pay cut? It's almost certain that when you retire you're going to have less income per month than before retirement, otherwise, why would you currently keep working? So, it's wise to "frontload" your premiums by paying more with pre-retirement dollars, which should make life insurance easier to afford.

By the way, we've designed plans for younger astute professionals where the portfolio (see the last chapter) has enough permanent life insurance at retirement to be able to quit paying premiums and yet have enough permanent life insurance to provide a survivor income large enough to choose the single life (max check) option, and no premiums during retirement!

Priority #5: Peace of Mind. The last priority is the most important—providing *peace of mind*. Once you have this problem solved, you're going to feel so good! You'll be able to say, "I have my financial plan in order because I have my pension option planning done." Too many people look at a financial plan—or they talk to their financial planner—and don't include this pension option planning. I believe it's one of the *most important* decisions in the financial world you'll ever make if you have a defined benefit pension. Granted, it does take some time to study the options and figure out if you can qualify for a plan, but it's very much worth it. Once you get this sorted out, you're going to feel so much better about your retirement outlook—you'll be in a much "die neater" spot.

By way of closing this chapter, here's a final caveat. Life insurance premiums are not tax deductible, and some people spend a lot of time wondering whether or not they should be buying policies if they can't deduct the cost. They figure they would rather put the monthly cost into their 401(k), 403(b), or 457 plan with pre-tax dollars. True, that would be pre-tax dollars, but the fact that it's contributed with pre-tax dollars means it's taxable later. On the other hand, while the life insurance premiums are not tax deductible, the eventual death benefit (the $1 million in our example) is income that is tax-free at death!

Which is better? Pre-tax or post-tax? If you're not sure, I want you to read the small book, *The Power of Zero*. In the book, author David McKnight will convince you that income taxes "have to go up" so paying more of your taxes today and putting money into "tax-free buckets" for later "tax-free" access is the way to go, without question. So as contrary as it may seem to some to *not* heavily invest in tax-deferred accounts today, it's better to go with future "tax-free" products such as life insurance and Roth IRAs. Read David McKnight's chapter "LIRP" (Life Insurance Retirement Plan) for more information. Also see my own "Retirement Pension Options" workbook via my website.[6]

I ask clients, "Would you rather pay taxes on the seed or the harvest?" A well-planned Pension Option Planning strategy will help you have a large lump of money, not subject to income tax, paid out later to your spouse to:

1. Buy an annuity equal to what the pension would have provided, or:

2. Take the lump sum and invest it with an adviser for lifetime income and a residual to the state, estate, heirs, or:

3. Pay off debts, or:

4. A combination of 1, 2, and 3.

In all of the death proceeds I've ever paid out, only a handful purchased the lifetime annuity. The rest did another comprehensive financial plan for survivors based on their needs, health, and goals at that time, maybe 20 years after

---

[6] Public Employees. https://retirementnationwide.com/

retirement. Whether you're a public employee or advisor, do what's best for the family.

CHAPTER 9

Death and Taxes – The Double-Whammy

Ben Franklin's famous quote says, "In this world nothing can be said to be certain, except death and taxes." Will Rogers then added on, saying, "The only difference between death and taxes is that death doesn't get worse every time Congress meets." We could go further, though, because taxation is even involved after your own death—even death can't stop taxation!

As taxes worsen (as Congress decides more often than not, even if it's not quite as sure as Will Rogers said) death can become an even greater financial burden to the family unaware of what we're calling the double-whammy of death and taxes. We've already talked about the inevitability of death (the 100% occurrence) in Chapter 4, let's further examine the link between death and taxes.

When I was younger, I used to think of death as the end. I had the wrong belief that if I died then there'd be no more taxes, right? Well, as I began to take classes and get various financial certifications, I began to realize just how ignorant I had been. Specifically, I learned that there is a tax classification called I.R.D., which means "Income with Respect to a Decedent."

This tax classification means the government can tax dead people—talk about grave robbing! Specifically, there's a final tax return you must file (well, somebody files it on the deceased person's behalf—you don't file it because you're dead, duh!). So when death inevitably gets us, taxes are right there to grab at us, too, and the government might grab a costly chunk if we're not properly prepared.

Estate Planning for the Wealthy

Even though income taxes are significant, the larger tax for many wealthy Americans is called "estate tax" (informally known as the "death tax"). These estate taxes are assessed on the value of what you leave behind after death. Basically, the IRS has decided that if you're wealthy enough, they're going to try to take a big chunk of money that you've already accumulated and likely already paid taxes on. Whether or not we like this policy of wealth redistribution to the government, there's no fighting the law (and the dead can't complain).

Speaking of the law, when I started in the business in 1983, the law was that if your net worth was over $600k

($1.2 million if married) you were exposed to estate taxes. Today, thankfully, the amounts are much higher. The current (2020) Federal estate taxes don't hit people until they are worth over $11 million personally or over $22 million per married couple (all the money below these amounts qualifies for an exemption). However, every state has their own "death tax" rules. In my state (Washington) the estate tax begins to hit you at $2 million personally and $4 million per married couple.

Thus, estate taxes are still something to consider and plan for because you never know if Congress (both the federal and state level) will change those laws (recall Will Rogers' warning) to massively lower the threshold for estate taxation. Even if the thresholds remain high and only touch the wealthy, having an understanding of the risk is part of "dying neatly."

To put the likelihood of estate taxation into perspective, every year I've been in business except for one solitary year, there has been some form of death tax. In case you're curious, the single year exception was 2010. What happened was the existing estate tax law expired and Congress didn't craft a new estate tax for that year.

A curious estate tax story is that of the famous New York Yankees team owner, George Steinbrenner. He was worth over $500 million and happened to pass away in 2010. It turned out to be the perfect time to pass away because his family never paid any estate taxes upon his death, which would have amounted to a massive tax bill of over $200 million. Talk about a lucky break! (Haven't *the Yankees* had enough good luck already over the years!?)

Despite the sensational story of George Steinbrenner, the odds are almost certain that wealthy people will have to pay some form of death taxes for the foreseeable future. So for most of us, this isn't a problem we have (sadly), but for the extremely wealthy the double-whammy of death and taxes can hit mind-numbingly hard.

Sure, Steinbrenner got incredibly lucky, but luck isn't how we ensure we die as neatly as possible. Besides, Congress could change the law at any time, and as a wise adviser once asked his clients, "Which tax law do you plan to die under?" Rather, you and your attorney would be wise to meet every so often to minimize death taxation and maximize wealth transfer to your heirs.

If you're in that top wealth category, you will inevitably die and be exposed to significant estate taxes that start at 40% of your money over $22 million (if married), unless before your death you find a way to give away this money through charity or the like.

Consider the following case study where life insurance can truly be the difference between someone who "bought the farm" and then lost the farm to the government (double whammy!) and someone who wisely plans and dies neatly.

Estate Planning "Wealthy" Business Owner Case Study

Suppose I have a client, a single business owner in Eastern Washington with a few thousand acres of wheat land worth $30,000,000 (land, equipment, livestock, real estate, and so on minus liabilities). He dies, and nine months after death the estate taxes (and state death tax) are due. Since he had no spouse or charitable interest, his tax exposure would be close to the following.

Federal tax: $30M - $11M = $19M. $19M x 40% = $7.6M.

State tax: $30M - $2M = $28M. $28M x 20% = $5.6M.

Total taxes due: $7.6M + $5.6M = $13.2M (due within 9 months after death).

However, the IRS is picky. They want *cash only*. No land, no stock or bonds, no equipment. I don't know any farmers who have $13.2 million in cash lying around. The IRS *doesn't care*! They might even loan it to you (Internal Revenue Code Section 6166). So what are your options?

1. **Cash** – $1 for each $1. Not likely.

2. **Bank loan** – $1.30 for each $1. Interest also.

3. **US Government financed (Section 6166)** – $1.40 for each $1. Probably higher interest.

4. **Permanent life insurance** – 2-3 cents for each $1. Leveraged money!

This fourth option employs a strategy that has been around for decades where you set up an Irrevocable Life Insurance Trust (ILIT) and gift the premiums to the trust so that death proceeds of $13.2 million (or more) will be liquid CASH at the time of death to pay some or all of these painful taxes. The ILIT keeps the proceeds out of the estate so you don't "compound" the problem by making the life insurance taxable. (Don't try this strategy without a qualified estate planning attorney.)

This strategy relates to Ben Feldman's famous "pennies on the dollar" saying. Consider the math on the purchase of a $10 million permanent life insurance policy with a $200,000/year premium. Divide $200,000 by $10 million and that's 2%, or 2 cents on the dollar. It's true that $200,000 is a lot of money to pay every year for premiums, but compared to $10 million it's only "pennies on the dollar."

Admittedly, an ILIT can get complicated, so if you're very wealthy (or plan on becoming so), it's essential to have a good estate planning attorney (and probably also a good CPA and a great life insurance agent) to help you set this

up. I highly recommend attorneys and CPAs who special-
ize in estate planning to get the "taxable estate" as small
as possible.

Like with my prior recommendations on agents, I also
highly recommend that your advisor has a CLU® (Char-
tered Life Advisor) degree from the American College or
partners with someone who has the strongest credentials
and products for your best interest.

On the topic of legal advice, let me emphatically state I am
not an attorney and do not practice law. Neither should
you try to practice law yourself unless you actually are an
attorney. Even so, attorneys should still be very careful,
because even many people in financial and legal professions fail to plan properly. For example, I have a good
friend who's an estate planning attorney over age 40 with
young children who is grossly under-insured and still
hasn't made any changes based on my many recommendations. "You can lead a horse to water, but you can't make
it drink."

For instance, in all of my experience in the life insurance
business, the stats are incredible: so few people have done
any will/trust planning. Even if you've been trained in
these topics, most people don't have a personal plan in
place to defend against the double-whammy. In fact, I've
found if people are under age 40, estate planning is so
rare, it's probably 1 in 20 (5%). At age 60 it's still only

about 1 in 5 (20%). This is shocking to me! Remember "the river in Egypt?" Death isn't deterred by your denial; neither will denial guard against taxation.

Why did I get my will? As I said earlier in this book I too used to be in "denial." I thought, "Why talk or plan for my death? It's a long way down the road and it's morbid." However, in 1983 I was under the mentorship of a great advisor, named Jim. He was really good at "painting the picture" of dying without adequate life insurance and no will, and the picture wasn't pretty.

He not only suggested, but pretty much demanded, that my wife and I get a will done. He urged that we take action to not only make sure that our money and assets go where we wanted if we both die, but to also set up guardianships for our young daughters, health care directives (to un-hook life support, for example), and durable powers of attorney (in case one of us were incapacitated—to make legal decisions). He also recommended a good attorney, whom I, in turn, recommended to many clients.

As a result of his powerful motivation, we took care of both estate planning and life insurance, and we felt so relieved that we did what was right in our planning. I had that *peace of mind* as a young husband and father—maybe it sounds trite but that feeling *was* priceless.

I've carried that peace of mind with me through all these past decades as my life has taken me from Spokane, Washington to Eugene, Oregon (11 years), Edina, Minnesota (7 years), Fresno, California (5 years), and back to Spokane, Washington as of 2016. Each state has its own probate laws, some are community property states, and every time I had to revise my will (I've revised it two times in the past 4 years).

Most of you won't have to update your will so often, but if you have minor children, you'll likely want to change the provisions to match your kids' changing needs. Especially important is once your children reach what the law calls "majority" (age 18). For instance, maybe you don't want to give such young adults a "pile of cash" too soon.

Think about how you water a lawn. Grass needs water, but you don't suddenly dump gallons of water on your yard. Rather, you use a measured pace through sprinklers to give what is needed, when it's needed. Likewise, your heirs need money to survive, but you don't want to overwhelm them. With proper planning through a trust you can "sprinkle" your money to your heirs over time.

So here you are reading this book and chances are you don't have a will or trust. Some people say everyone has a will: it's the state's version. That's not true, with no will you will die "intestate" (pronounced "in-tes-tate"), which is a legal term that simply means "without a will." So what?

Dying "intestate" can create several problems, such as being subjected to what's known as probate. This is a slow, tedious process of proving who has claim to what, which is carried out through probate court. The whole process, including all transfers of legal title of assets, can take 18-36 months depending on the state. Without proper estate planning, houses, other real estate, stocks, bonds, contracts, and more all have to go through probate and the court decides the legal heirs. It's public, costly, painful, and takes far too long.

Many assets don't go through probate, like joint bank accounts, property owned jointly (joint tenants), beneficiary arrangements of IRAs, 401(k) plans, life insurance, etc. These assets go to the beneficiaries shortly after death with no government intervention. But is that what you want?

One piece of planning that I did (with good advice from my attorney) was to create a "testamentary trust" for my children's college education funded by life insurance. Upon my death, my wife would become the trustee, but that money could *only* be used for education or health benefits (not her trips to Hawaii with her new boyfriend 😊).

Building on my personal story, I often ask a client if he or she wants to guarantee education money for his or her children (and grandchildren) whether the client lives, dies, or becomes disabled. The client almost always says, "Yes!" In order to establish this education fund, you need a life insurance policy with a rider called "disability waiver of premium" set up with the beneficiary being a trust so that money is "locked up" for the children.

By channeling the money (death proceeds) into a trust, the money can only be used for post-high school education, vocational training, or medical emergencies. The children can't just go to Costa Rica with a pile of money and become beach bums (we want to wisely sprinkle money, not haphazardly dump it). Another bonus to this great plan is, it doesn't count as an asset and affect your FAFSA[7] score like a 529 plan[8] does for financial aid.

Let's get back to the probate problem. Suppose you own a business and a home, and you and your spouse tragically die together in an accident. What happens? The business and home will eventually (after probate) transfer to your

---

[7] FAFSA®: Apply for Aid. Federal Student Aid. https://studentaid.ed.gov/sa/fafsa

[8] An Introduction to 529 Plans. U.S. Securities and Exchange Commission. https://www.sec.gov/reportspubs/investor-publications/investorpubsintro529htm.html

children. But what if they are minors? Then the court will transfer title of the business and home to a custodial account and appoint a guardian for your children. The custodial account managers and guardian are supposed to be trustworthy and only make decisions in the best interest of the children, but abuse and neglect can often happen.

Regardless of the quality of the overseers, when your oldest child turns 18 and says, "Yippie, I'm no longer a minor," he or she gets the portion entitled to him or her at 18 years old! Are you "ok" with that? Personally, my children are age 40 and 37, and I still wouldn't want them to run my business or be given a lot of money all at one time! (Sorry girls—I still love you!)

Unfortunately, without proper estate planning, this sudden transfer of wealth will occur when the government dictates. This transfer includes your 401(k) plan, life insurance, cash in the bank, and so on. As stated, all of the assets will be controlled by the state as long as your children are minors. Ever since I was a young father, I've hated this scenario of a government stranger in control of my children's financial fate. Even though this plan is not in place for me personally since my girls are grown now, here's what I set up in the past together with a good life insurance company.

If either my wife or I died, all of the assets would go to the survivor, except for the testamentary education trust for the children (or grandchildren). If we both died, part of the money would go to charity (see Chapter 10) and the balance would go to a trust for the children's well-being and private secondary school if desired (while they were minors). Upon graduation from high school, the provisions of the trust would pay for college or trade school, including room and board, but not just for living expenses without schooling. The idea was to motivate them to get educated or trained if they wanted more money.

Once the youngest reached age 25, 25% of the trust corpus (a legal term meaning the asset value of the trust used to produce income) was to be dispersed in cash to them. At age 30, 33% of the remaining corpus was to be dispersed and at age 35 the balance would be dispersed. I'm not saying this arrangement is ideal. I'm just saying it was at least a plan put in place to ensure I had a say in my children's financial futures if tragedy struck.

I have revised that 3 times since then because my daughters are now 40 and 37 and I have 3 grandchildren. My current plan after the death of my wife and myself is for a portion (10%) to still go to charity. The other 90% of the assets go into a trust, and the principal can only be dipped into for education (children, grandchildren, and great grandchildren) and health costs not covered by health insurance (including things like clinical trials).

Each year, 2% of the corpus (principal) will be split between my two daughters. Once they're both deceased, the amount will go to 4% for their children and 6% for the children's children. If the money is invested properly, the corpus should continue to grow at least through my great grandchildren's generations. My wife and I will be long gone, but the legacy will continue (see Chapter 10).

I'm not saying you should follow my personal plans outlined above, but it gives you an idea of what "dying neatly" looks like for lessening the double-whammy of death and taxes and actually turning your demise into blessings for future generations. From this starting point, get some great ideas from your attorney and create your own "estate plan" custom-tailored for you.

This chapter could be a lot longer and include many details of wills, trusts, legal issues upon death, etc. But that's why I highly recommend you do your research and find a great attorney whom you trust, who specializes in estate planning. After you've set up a comprehensive estate plan, review and modify it periodically.

As a side note, if you're wealthy, if you or your spouse die separately, upon the first death you might want to consider transferring some assets to an ILIT (Irrevocable Life Insurance Trust) or a spousal trust. This is where my legal advice stops. Rely on a good attorney to help you here. Please don't use the internet. That's like having your doctor or dentist online in the virtual world working on your body or teeth remotely—it might work, but the risk isn't worth it.

"People don't plan to fail; they fail to plan." You don't have to be one of these people, though.

Having finished the bulk of our estate planning discussion, most of you will likely see the wisdom in such planning and perhaps say, "That really makes sense—I should do that." However, life can sidetrack us all. We get busy, procrastinate, and put things off indefinitely. I understand. Remember, back in 1983 my mentor had to very strongly push me to get my own estate planning taken care of and I am still grateful today for his guidance.

In that same spirit, after presenting the material in this chapter to my clients, I proactively ask them if they think the next 30-60 days is enough time to get this very important planning completed. Usually they say, "Yes," and with diligence and my prodding, they get it completed. Afterward, they invariably thank me for being persistent because they, too, have a *peace of mind* about their estate.

It really is true—as much as things change, they stay the same. You, too, can have that same good feeling I've felt since 1983 if you'll take the same steps as me and so many others to "die neatly" and lessen the burden of the "double whammy" of death and taxes. More importantly, I guarantee that whatever the cost, the peace of mind will be worth it.

CHAPTER 10

Legacy Planning – Gifts After Death

Legacy planning is about leaving assets to others or institutions upon your death. This charitable giving is one of the most rewarding and impactful choices you can make in your life, and the benefits extend far beyond the financial. If putting your own family's finances in order for after your death is "dying neatly," then establishing a charitable legacy allows you to "die *extra* neatly." Let me explain.

Rotary International is one of the largest philanthropic non-profit organizations in the world with over 1.2M members and 35,000 clubs worldwide. I have been a member for over 35 years in six separate clubs in five states, and I've never met so many people giving of their time, money, and talent. They come from different political origins, religious backgrounds, careers, ages, economic backgrounds, and yet they all live by the great motto "service above self."

As great as the organization is, less than 1% of their memberships are members of the Bequest Society. This subgroup pledges at least $10,000 to the Rotary Foundation after their death. That means over 99% of members don't pledge to donate from their estate (or pledge less than $10,000). I know there are countless people who give "off the record" to Rotary upon their death, but why not commit to that in writing? Your kids may not have the same charitable desire once they inherit your money.

Out of these strong convictions, for my entire Rotary career, I have been on the Foundation Committee, and I have always been baffled by how few members commit to the Bequest Society. It just requires a signature on one piece of paper and a pledge to "carve out" some of your estate to one of the best non-profit organizations in the world.

Whether it's Rotary, The Lion's Club, Kiwanis, your church, a school or university, or thousands of other great causes that need money, you could help serve the world through what we call "legacy planning." (Rotarians, please talk to your Foundation Director and get the one page form or visit the website to become a Bequest Society member today.)

When I'm talking with my estate planning clients (many who are wealthy and have already donated tens of thousands of dollars to charity), I ask them if they have a charitable legacy plan. "What does that mean?" they inquire. I respond, "Do you want to leave a portion of your estate to charities of your choice and create a charitable foundation that will last long after your death?" Most clients are intrigued. "Tell me more," they say.

This concept is about "tithing your estate," which means committing to at least 10% of your assets upon your death to be pledged to charities. Many people already give (tithe) to charity (or church) while they're alive, so we're talking about including charity in your final financial act in this life. If charity has been a special and fulfilling part of your life, then give it a formal and fulfilling part of your life after death.

While some clients won't be interested, many other clients are very interested and change their estate plans to accommodate their renewed desires for charity. Many tell me that they never thought of making charity part of their estates—their legacies—and are glad to explore this option in their planning.

Why doesn't everyone do this? Why do 99% of Rotarians not commit to the Bequest Society legacy plan? Many of the reasons why were discussed earlier in the book, including denial, procrastination, fear, or simply being unaware (they just haven't heard about it).

In fact, I think most people fall into the last category. So many good people love their family and want to maximize the amount that goes to their children and as little to taxes as possible, and this focus means they haven't considered the charitable "legacy plan."

For your legacy plan, I suggest giving 10% of your estate to charity. This setup can be done easily with an attorney who can help design a will or trust to accommodate this arrangement.

Think about the numbers. 10% isn't that much. 90% still goes to your family. Mathematically, your beneficiaries or survivors will still get nine times more (the other 90%) than you're giving away. 90% is a big percentage, and the total dollar amount is still going to be a big number. See the diagram below.

DIAGRAM: "Tithing Your Estate" – 10% and 90%

Estate Size	To Charity	To Family
$100,000	$10,000	$90,000
$250,000	$25,000	$225,000
$500,000	$50,000	$450,000
$1,000,000	$100,000	$900,000
$10,000,000	$1,000,000	$9,000,000
$50,000,000	$5,000,000	$45,000,000
etc.	etc.	etc.

Think of a child saying, "I should have gotten the money, not that charity!" No, your children should feel honored that you gave 10% (or more) to a worthy cause. I can't imagine if I inherited money from my family (none expected, sadly) that I would ever question their charitable desires.

Both of my daughters know our desire and plan for legacy planning, and they support the plan. I also hope my example will instill a charitable mindset in them for their own future estates. Remember, inheritance is a gift from you, not a requirement. It's from your heart, and even if you give half of it away to charity, that other half is still an unearned gift to your heirs.

I have a lot of respect for the Giving Pledge[9] project. It's a club started by some of the wealthiest people in the world like Bill Gates and Warren Buffett, who started the club in 2010. There are over 170 members who are billionaires and commit to give at least half of their estates to charity. Sometimes we complain that the wealthy are taking too much and they have a disproportionate share of the wealth in America, and yet these great leaders are giving hundreds of billions of dollars to charity. Many have created foundations like The Bill and Melinda Gates Foundation that is already funded with over $50 billion in assets. They have given billions each year to that charity. They are already some of the most philanthropic people in the world.

As Rotarians, they have given over a billion dollars to the Rotary Foundation to help eradicate polio. At the time of this printing there were only 3 countries left in the world with cases of polio. Their foundation is also committed to world sanitation projects like sewage treatment and self-sustaining toilets. There are many world-changing projects that this foundation is committed to. Without Bill

---

[9] The Giving Pledge. https://givingpledge.org/

and Melinda Gates, Warren Buffet, and hundreds of thousands of other givers, all this wouldn't happen.

My wife Debbie and I are moved by philanthropy too, and have committed at least 10% of our estate to charitable needs. My original plan was that part of my life insurance policy would go to charity. But after studying the impact of qualified money in IRAs, 401(k) plans, etc., we changed the beneficiary of our Bequest Society membership and other charitable donations that come out of our pre-tax bucket so that the charitable portion becomes "never-taxed" dollars.

The proceeds or death benefits of our life insurance then will go to my family or kids, tax-free. The IRAs, or pre-tax dollars, would go to retirement, and the balance to my estate and charities. My estate will have to pay income taxes on the "pre-tax" dollars, but the non-profit charities won't pay taxes since they'll receive "never-taxed" dollars. Please consider this tax-leveraged approach to charitable bequests.

The IRS encourages charitable giving by letting you deduct up to 50% of your Adjusted Gross Income (AGI) each year on your income tax return. Upon death, the IRS has two unlimited clauses where you can avoid all federal estate taxes, which are some of the largest taxes in America today. For every $1.00 of your estate over $22M, $0.40 (40%) goes to the IRS without proper planning.

Two Unlimited Deductions from Federal Estate Taxes

1. **The unlimited marital deduction.** You can give all of your estate to your spouse and pay no federal or state taxes on the death of the first spouse (under current tax laws). Although this seems like a great idea, you are just postponing the inevitable and if you are wealthy and pay taxes or subject to estate taxes (an estate over $22M), you may still have estate taxes due upon the death of the second spouse. There are also some tax planning strategies that may be worth paying some of the taxes or transferring money to a trust upon the first death. Good estate planning attorneys are recommended here. This is what they specialize in, and your estate/heirs could possibly save a lot of future estate taxes.

2. **Unlimited charitable deductions.** You can give as much as you want to most charities and pay zero federal or state taxes on that money. Think about those billionaires. They have a massive estate tax liability unless they plan to give billions away free from estate taxes. I would bet Bill and Melinda Gates give over 90% of their almost $100 billion net worth to charity. Good for them! I

would wager that these charities will be better stewards of the money than the U.S. government!

To reiterate, most who read this book will not have any future estate tax liability. At the time of printing, if you're married, federal estate taxes can be avoided up to about $22M net worth. Still, it may pay to seek advice from a good estate planning attorney since the fees you pay to them may be quite minor relative to the possible major tax bills down the road if you don't plan.

Also note that you have to put your charitable desires in *writing*. The IRS won't assume you wanted to give any money away because they'd rather have the tax income!

I've previously mentioned one of my great mentors, Marty Polhemus, and how he taught me so much about Human Life Value (remember the "money machine" example from Chapter 5). But Marty was also one of the most loving, philanthropic people I have ever met. When he died in 2015, there were over 1,500 people in attendance at his funeral, including family members, friends, community leaders, most of all the agents, former agents, and their families, like me and my family, who were motivated, led, taught, and coached into successful life insurance careers.

What amazed me most about Marty was his passion for charity, specifically his love for Whitworth University (a small, private Christian college in Spokane, Washington). He raised a mammoth amount of money for the Whitworth Foundation. He was on the foundation board and helped donors with two major charitable strategies.

1. Buying Life Insurance Policies. If policy holders from his company had old life insurance policies that the owner wanted to surrender or cash out, he would ask them if they would like to sell their policy (and end up with the same amount of money) to the Whitworth Foundation. Most people would say "yes" (because they receive the same amount of money), so then Marty would buy the person's policy for the Whitworth Foundation.

Think about that. The foundation is now the owner, payer, and beneficiary of a life insurance policy on all these people, guaranteeing a payout in the future much greater than the purchase price. For Whitworth, Marty helped raise tens of millions of dollars as inevitable (as death always is, see Chapter 3) future endowments for the foundation.

For example, take a $100,000 life insurance policy with a $30,000 cash value. The foundation would pay the owner $30,000, but then the foundation would be the beneficiary of the inevitable $100,000. So for $30,000, they would end up with $100,000 sometime in the future when (not "if") the insured dies. The foundation just had to set up a tracking system, so they'd find out when someone died.

2. Donating Premiums. Another strategy Marty employed was to have a charitable donor take out a new life insurance policy and donate the premiums to the foundation. The foundation would immediately become the owner, payer, and beneficiary of the policy (like in the first strategy). The premiums would be paid for with the donor's (insured person's) tax deductible donation (within IRS limits).

Here's an example: The donor starts a new life insurance policy by taking a physical exam and is insured with a $500,000 death benefit. The foundation purchases a permanent life insurance policy with a premium of $10,000 per year. Even though it's the foundation applying for the policy, the donor is the one who has to prove insurability. The donor agrees to donate to the foundation an amount of money equal to the $10,000 premium, so the foundation can put that into the life insurance policy.

Technically, this donation has to be considered unrestricted because it's a "gift" to the foundation (they can't be obligated to use it for premiums), but it ends up being a very good choice by the foundation directors to use this money for the premium payments. Therefore, the foundation would be the owner, and if the person decided not to donate to the foundation at some point, the foundation just has to find another source of premium dollars in the future or surrender the policy.

Both of these charitable strategies may seem complex and confusing, but wise advisors (following in Marty's footsteps) can navigate these powerful legacy planning techniques. Indeed, Marty was brilliant and ahead of his time in the 1970s and 1980s when he was utilizing these strategies. He called these "leveraged gifts."

Today, thousands of churches, schools, and non-profit organizations are using the overall strategy of leveraging future death benefits and leveraging gifts for future "inevitable gains." Many non-profits give recognition for this incredible donation. The donor gets the satisfaction of knowing that his or her gift of "legacy" with a "leveraged gift" is far more over time than just the yearly donations.

This is where a discussion with the foundation director and your estate planning attorney are the smartest way to put this plan together. Make sure you also have an experienced life insurance agent and a company with over 120 years of experience with a proven track record so the company will be around long after you're physically gone but remain "in legacy."

On a more personal scale, my father-in-law died of cancer in 1982. He was a great man and the only real father I'd ever known. My wife and I were only married six years at that time and had just welcomed our second daughter into the world. My wife was really close to her dad, who had suffered tremendously for the previous year and a half with pancreatic cancer. This was a devastating family time for us, and I tried to be supportive as best I knew how. I also became very passionate about cancer research.

Cancer is a brutal disease that takes millions of lives each year and with this personal loss in my life, I felt compelled to donate money to cancer research. I had an office in northern Idaho at the time, and the Kootenai Medical Center Foundation was raising money for cancer research through charitable life insurance policies.

So I agreed to buy one of these policies and also help other donors do the same. The life insurance policy the foundation owns on me requires a $1,000 annual premium and provides a $100,000 death benefit. Think about those numbers. It only costs me 1% of the payout per year (and I can "tax deduct" the premium each year) for Kootenai to get $100,000 upon my death. I feel really good about that leverage.

Granted, they are still waiting for the payout (because I'm still ticking!), but I also feel really good knowing part of my legacy is guaranteed money paid in honor of my father-in-law to help prevent others from suffering so much. Plus, the foundation has access to the cash value of the policy as a growing asset for use before I die. So if you're charitable, healthy, and want to leverage your donation to a charity of your choice upon your death, consider this fantastic option.

Let me also mention that there are more complicated leverage gifts like Charitable Remainder Trusts (CRTs). There are also Charitable Lead Trusts (CLTs), private annuities, etc. I don't need to get into the details because all this can be explained and set up by a good estate planning attorney and help from the charitable foundation working together to fulfill your desires.

In summary, "dying neatly," in my mind, includes gifts after death, and I hope that you feel in your heart the urge to set up some form of charitable gift upon your death. Don't we all strive to raise a family that loves? So why not leave a "legacy of love" through well-laid legacy planning? So why not "tithe your estate" with the same (or maybe even greater) open-hearted giving you engage in today?

Whether you set up charitable trusts or donate life insurance premiums or simply volunteer to help raise money while you're alive, legacy planning should be part of everyone's estate plan. We all know you can't take it with you, so let this be your final act of modeling charity to your beloved heirs.

They may inherit the bulk of your money, but they also get to share in your charitable spirit one final time. These charities, however, need people like you and me to plan while we're still alive and productive, so they can continue helping others after we're long gone. Maybe your actions will even inspire and motivate multiple generations of your own family to become more charitably-minded themselves. That's a pretty "neat" way to leave this world, isn't it?

CHAPTER 11

Long-Term Disability – The Living Death

We've already talked about the reality of death, but sometimes tragedy leads to something other than death. Sometimes your "money machine" (the ability to create an income—from Chapter 5) doesn't simply die. Rather, it can sputter or run out of gas for a while. This is known as disability because you no longer have the ability to provide like you could before. I call this situation the living death because your old productive life dies, but you have to go on living with whatever resources are available. So how do you prepare for disability using the principles of "dying neatly?" Let's begin with a story.

Years ago, I had a client who owned a radiator repair shop and bought life insurance and disability insurance on himself as well as putting together a good retirement plan. He was physically active and healthy in his mid-40s but had a motorcycle (my nurse friend calls them "donor-cycles" thanks to their mortality risk).

While driving his motorcycle in an urban area of town a car pulled out in front of him and he crashed into the side of the car and flew over the car. After hitting the ground like a ragdoll, he rolled over several times and lay there. Luckily, he was wearing a helmet.

I didn't find out about the accident until 5 months later when he called me. He had suffered migraine headaches, broken bones, and back strain. His doctor said that he could only work 4 hours per day. When I met with him he shared that he had to go to his radiator shop or it would have to close!

Fortunately, he purchased a good disability insurance policy with a partial disability feature that paid 50% for 6 months even with no loss of income, then it was based on income loss. We filed a claim and the insurance company went back 2 months (90 day waiting period, plus 2 months took him to 5 months). The company paid 50% of his salary for the next 4 months and then continued to pay 50% disability for the next 5 years, over which time he was able to work half-time. Many companies have similar policies of "strict underwriting but liberal claims." (The residual or partial disability feature is paramount because most claims are not for total disability.)

If it wasn't for this, he would have lost his business, his ability to earn income, probably his home and maybe his marriage. When he bought the policy from me, I asked him, "What is the most valuable asset that you own?" Like most people over 36 years that I asked that question, the answer is usually "my home."

After a quick discussion, he agreed it was his "ability to earn income" (Chapter 5's Human Life Value). The problem with being disabled is that it is a "living death." Your ability to earn a full income has "died," but we still have to feed you, clothe you, rehabilitate you, etc., which all cost money. You may come back and become efficient again, but you may not. Think about the following two choices regarding purchasing disability income protection. You have the choice of Job A or Job B:

Job A – *$100,000/year, if disabled: income = $0*

Job B – *$98,000/year, if disabled: income = $60,000/year*

If you picked Job B, you just purchased a disability income insurance policy that costs $2,000 per year in premiums and provides $60,000 per year ($5,000 per month) if you become disabled. This is wise, important planning. Protecting your HLV (Human Life Value) is the most important insurance you will ever buy, and this insurance includes both life *and* disability insurance.

DIAGRAM: Disability insurance – Before and After a Disability

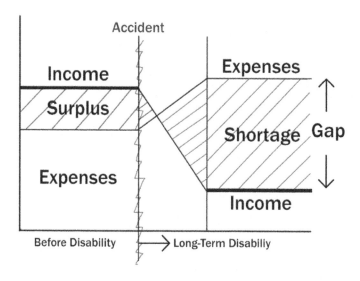

Disability insurance is important and necessary, especially if you have a high paying "white collar" job like a doctor, dentist, attorney, or engineer where there's little chance of disability occurring, but a huge loss if it happens. Professions like construction, plumbing, and landscaping have a higher probability of occurrence. Therefore, the premium is usually really high and benefits can be limited, so it's likely not worth purchasing because it's too expensive relative to your income. Plus, some occupations simply can't be insured (coded as RNA, Risk Not Available).

Let me share a story about a relative of mine, whom we'll call Sally. Sally was a high-level retail manager for a large retail store. She began working her way up as a teenager, paid her way through college, and continued to climb the corporate ladder through her early career years. Along the way she got married. Her husband happened to be a life insurance agent and was smart enough to get her both life and disability insurance.

As life would have it, Sally became disabled at age 38, with two very young girls at home. Given her condition, her doctor said that she could *never* work retail management again, which was all she had known for so many years. Fortunately, she had an "own occupation" rider on her disability policy, which said if you "can't perform the principal duties of your occupation due to accident or illness, you are disabled." At the time of this printing she is still disabled through this policy beyond age 50 because she still cannot work fulltime in her "own occupation" (retail management at the time of the disability).

She and her husband bought a good policy that will pay her to age 65, and they have been able to raise their two girls with access to private schools, college, and more. It took a sacrifice to pay those premiums before her disability, but you can be sure they're glad they made a plan all those years ago and kept good disability insurance!

Even though disability insurance is so crucial, it can be the most confusing, misunderstood insurance you will ever purchase. Most agents don't sell disability insurance, either because their companies don't offer it or it's too confusing. There are disability insurance brokers in major metropolitan areas who can "shop" companies for you or your advisors. Get references and compare. Make sure your advisor is experienced in the arena or find another one. Your advisor may be really good at investments and money management but weaker on "risk management planning" like life insurance, disability insurance, and long-term care insurance. It's okay and even recommended to have more than one advisor, "defense" and "offense."

I don't believe in paying extra premiums for short-term disability because once the short term runs out, if you're still disabled, the income still is gone, and those premiums can be better allocated toward the savings needed for emergencies. Economists say you should have 3-6 months *coverable* in this account.

My philosophy is protect to age 65 (maybe 67) or lifetime with a 90 days elimination period (deductible). If you can afford it, add an inflation rider and also APB (Additional Purchase Benefit) to guarantee additional coverage. Insurance should only be to cover those catastrophic losses: medical expenses, premature death, disability income protection, long-term care expenses, and home/auto/liability insurance. I cannot recommend expensive maintenance insurance, short-term disability, or accident/cancer policies. Put that money into an HSA or FSA account (pre-tax money) to pay the deductible on your medical insurance. Again, get a qualified advisor involved here.

This complicated purchase can be done wrong so I recommend a Disability Insurance (DI) broker who can shop several companies and depending on occupation class and desired coverage find you the best deal. If you are loyal to one insurance company, make sure that they are highly rated (by AM Best, Moody's, Standard & Poor's) and have decades of proven track record. Don't be afraid to compare two or three or more companies (and agents) yourself.

Google "high rated" disability insurance carriers and compare. With adequate life and disability insurance coverage you should feel really comfortable about your "defensive financial plan," except the last "human" risk of long-term care. Past the age of 65, there's a 70% chance of spending 90 days or longer in a nursing facility or home care. The next chapter will deal with this expensive life changing circumstance.

CHAPTER 12

Long-Term Care Planning – Asset Depletion or Protection?

Long-term care is different from long-term disability. Long-term disability, as discussed in the prior chapter, is for loss of income due to injury or illness, but you may still be able to take care of yourself. Long-term care, on the other hand, says you are unable to perform your own normal, daily living functions. This care need can be due to physical problems or cognitive impairment, such as dementia or Alzheimer's disease.

To illustrate the devastating impact of long-term care needs, let's return to the tragic story of my brother Mike that we began at the end of Chapter 4 (Denial). At the age of 22, he was in a horrible motorcycle accident and ended up in a coma (I was only 21). Now, as we begin to discuss long-term care, the time has finally come to conclude Mike's painful story.

What I didn't say before was that Mike's accident caused him to suffer intense traumatic brain injury, and there were very little signs that he would ever recover. However, he hung on to life for a year through the life support machines, and each day visiting him was agony, as hope kept slipping away.

But life had to go on for me. Being in the Air Force Academy, I had to go back to school, and in the meantime, the hospital had to transfer him to a nursing home since his condition wasn't improving. Even worse, our family didn't have money for a private facility, so Mike was shipped off to a state funded nursing home.

Two months later I came home from school, newly engaged to my fiancée, and I transferred to a local college in town, Whitworth College (now Whitworth University). My fiancée (now my wife since 1976!) and I visited Mike at first a couple times a week, then once a week, then every 10 days or so.

This visiting went on month after month, as Mike continued to "live" but decay before our eyes. His demise became more and more inevitable and it became harder to see this healthy 170-pound, "studly" 22-year-old dwindle down to about 90 pounds of skin and bones.

On a personal note, I, myself, became very traumatized by this soul-crushing nursing home experience. Walking through the stench of the nursing home past older people afflicted by strokes or with dementia, screaming out, to get to the end of the hallway to see Mike was almost unbearable. To this day the memories are still too real.

After a year or so, the inevitable happened, and Mike died, still in that coma from that catastrophic day on his motorcycle. Truthfully, when he died, we all felt relief—at least the agony of his weight loss and lack of response was over. I also choose to believe he had final peace with God in his final days.

Why do I bring up Mike's story again? The reason is to highlight the crucial importance of long-term care by vividly conveying the reality of many nursing homes. Trust me, you do *not* want to die in a "state funded" facility, and the reality of nursing homes doesn't just apply to 80 or 90-year-olds—my brother died at age 22 after a year in that coma in that bleak and ugly place. I never want another loved one to experience that "exit strategy" for life. Mike did not "die neatly!"

I'm not trying to attack "state funded" facilities. Much of their problems are out of their control since most of them are grossly underfunded, meaning they are understaffed and under-deliver proper care. So if your plan is to depend on the "state" to put you in a nursing home, remember a few things:

1. **Poverty.** You have to be on Medicaid (welfare) to qualify. That means you've spent all of your assets except a couple thousand dollars (the amount can change every year). After the state takes your 401(k) plan, investments, and many other valuables to offset their costs, then they pay it all.

2. **Limits.** Medicare doesn't cover nursing homes except for the first 100 days. Then they only pay the portion over $100/day. That's only 3 months and 10 days, which is almost nothing compared to how long most people need. The average stay is about three years.

3. **Experience.** Before you accept that as a default, go visit a couple of lower end "state funded" facilities and ask yourself, "Is this 'dying neatly?'" (I can't even walk into a nursing home 44 years after Mike's death.)

Planning for this "probability" (not possibility) can be costly and takes time, and most people don't want to "die in a nursing home." I've heard every excuse/reason to not purchase some type of long-term care coverage. Let's go through a few, starting with a big one.

1. **"My family will take care of me."** My first response is, "Is that what you want? To have your family become burdened with 24-hour care for you?" My youngest daughter

was a professional caregiver for two years. One for an elderly woman who had a stroke and the other for a quadriplegic 37-year-old man who was a motivational speaker. She worked full time (or more) in both cases and cleaned, bathed, took them to the bathroom, and fed them, among many other trying duties.

With all of that talent, even though now married with 3 beautiful children, my daughter said to me, "Dad I hope you didn't buy any long-term care insurance because I'll take care of you." I don't know about you, but I don't want my daughter bathing, cleansing, or cleaning my behind! I own a lot of long-term care insurance so I can keep my dignity and not be a burden to Jodi, my wife, or others close to me!

However, I did tell Jodi that she can be my "care coordinator" rather than the "care giver." Even with much insurance, it's very important to have a trusted person (like an adult child) to make sure you're receiving proper care. Remember, the reason you need to use long-term care is because you're in a diminished state, so with proper insurance your family can be unburdened by the giving of the care but still feel useful in the coordinating of the care.

They can make sure that you're receiving the kind of care you would want while hiring someone else to do the messy and ugly jobs. This frees your family up to spend quality time with you. They can be compassionately present with you and the family without distractions.

2. **"Long-Term Care insurance is really expensive! (The premiums are really high!)"** This is true, and you have to purchase it while you're younger and healthy. The younger and healthier you are, the lower the premium. I pay over $600/month for my wife and I, but if you're under age 60 and healthy, you can still find affordable premiums. Think of these premiums as "asset protection" insurance. I tell clients, "The premium is not the problem, the problem is 'self-insurance.'" If this happens, the costs can devastate even the best planned investment portfolios.

Take one example. The average stay in an Alzheimer's facility is 2-3 years before death, and in 2020 the cost, even in a smaller city, can be over $10k per month! Big cities will be even more. Using our monthly number, let's assume 2.5 years (30 months) of long-term care. Thirty months times $10k is $300k! If I paid premiums for 20 years (at my $600 per month amount for my wife and I) it could be less than half of that cost ($600/month is $7,200/year, which is $144,000 in 20 years).

With most Americans having their money in tax-deferred instruments (like 401(k) plans, IRAs, 403(b) accounts, etc.), in order to come up with $300k you need $400k pretax (assuming a 25% tax bracket) out of your hard-saved retirement dollars. The reason for this is that the long-term care costs are paid with "after tax" dollars. You can't "tax deduct" $10,000 a month! Even with $1M in an IRA, 40% ($400k) is a big hit to pay for long-term care.

The key is to "leverage your dollars" and pay "pennies on the dollar" for this highly probable, extremely expensive occurrence. After age 65 there is a 70% chance of collecting on a long-term care policy and a 90% chance of either the husband or wife collecting. Remember how we want to only purchase insurance for catastrophic losses with much risk? That's a risk worth insuring, if you qualify.

3. "What if I pay all of these premiums and die without ever having a claim?" Everyone knows someone who this happened to and honestly, I fear it too, but I rationalize it like auto insurance, homeowner's insurance, or liability insurance. I may never have a claim there either or maybe small claims compared to premiums paid. Remember, we insure to "transfer risk" and have "peace of mind."

Even my plan at $600 a month ($7,200 a year) with a couple of premium increases in 25 years, I could pay over $250,000! I still believe it's worth the cost so I can pass more money to my children upon death. If you have the ability to pay the steep costs, you should come out ahead eventually, unless you die quickly after needing care or are blessed to die without prolonged medical needs.

At the time of this book's printing, the most common rec-ommendation for long-term care planning is a "hybrid" plan. It is a life insurance policy with a LTC or CCB (Chronic Care Benefit) rider. This is still "leveraged money" (remember, pennies on the dollar), but we know the inevitable occurrence is death so the "tax-free" dollars from the life insurance will inevitably be paid (if it's funded properly—review regularly).

The LTC or CCB rider is just an "advance on the death ben-efit" and the proceeds are just subtracted and a lien (an ownership interest) is taken against the inevitable death benefit. For example, it might be a $500,000 policy and $200,000 was advanced for LTC expenses before death. Then at death the balance $300,000 (minus interest from "advance" until death) is paid out "income tax-free" to the beneficiary or beneficiaries. By the way, I don't believe in adding riders where you pay up front because you may just die without a long-term care claim. Then the death benefit would be less for the beneficiary, just like buying a separate long-term care policy.

4. "Should I pay recurring premiums or a single pre-mium for this hybrid policy?" This is more of a prefer-ence than math because insurance companies give big discounts for upfront money. The question is really your "opportunity cost" of tying up money. For example, would you rather pay $10,000 per year for 20 years or pay

$130,000 up front? The $10,000 x 20 years = $200,000, but with the "time value of money" (today's dollars are worth more than tomorrow's) it might be a wash.

One other disadvantage of paying a large lump into a life insurance policy is that you will lose some important tax advantages. The IRS has what they call a "7-pay" test, and they limit the amount of premium that can be contributed in the first 7 years, or the policy becomes a MEC (Modified Endowment Contract). The good news is that a MEC still has a tax-free death benefit and LTC benefits. The bad news is that other withdrawals from the cash value can be partially taxable and if you're younger than 59 ½ include a 10% penalty. Also, with a MEC, loans from normal life insurance policies, which are generally "tax-free," can be taxable and include the penalty (as mentioned above) if taken before age 59½.

A well-designed life insurance (permanent) policy still provides tax-free access to cash or loans for living benefits like educational costs, mortgage payoffs, and business opportunities. I loaned a trusted business partner a bunch of money to help him buy a business. Where did I get the money from? I got it from policy loans from my cash value life insurance policies.

As my business partner pays me back, I pay the policy back. It's a great arrangement, and I was honored to be able to help out a friend. This was all possible thanks to careful planning on my part, which has been blessing others even before I get old. Plus, since the business I loaned the money to is a hardware store, I get to buy tools (and toys) at cost for the next 8 years (I need to negotiate an extension on that benefit ☺). A good life insurance professional can help you sort all of this out. Whether it's a lump sum payment or recurring premiums, these hybrid policies will help you with the three possibilities discussed before:

1. **Hope for the Best.** Live a long time and die in your sleep without suffering. The beneficiaries get all of the death benefit "income tax-free," and you can access the money early for vacations, loans to children, and even tax-free LIRPs (unless it's a MEC)!

2. **Prepare for the Worst.** Whether premature death, terminal illness, chronic care, or critical care, the money is there for all of those with good policies.

3. **Take what Comes with Gratitude.** You can't control most things in life, but you can endure minor losses. Be content knowing that you have a "plan" to protect against catastrophic losses, which could drain your investment portfolio (and maybe ruin you).

To quote Rick Hayes, CLU®, ChFC®, CLF, a regional life specialist with New York Life, "Permanent life insurance is the best financial tool in America today." The money grows tax deferred, is accessible tax-free, and in many states is untouchable by creditors. Then upon death you receive a huge balloon of "leveraged money" (i.e. money paid "income tax-free" to your beneficiaries). You can also get a good yield on your money with very little risk. All in all, that's a pretty "neat" way to die, isn't it?

(Make sure one of your advisors is passionate and knowledgeable about life insurance, long-term care, and disability income planning. If your advisor doesn't want to discuss these issues, keep him or her as your "offensive coordinator" and hire a specialist to be your "defensive coordinator" (as discussed in Chapter 2). Go to LifeHappens.org for more information like materials, videos, and calculators.)

CHAPTER 13

Faith – Don't Die Without It

So far, this book has mostly been about finances and philosophy. I've shared diagrams and numbers and tried to tie everything together with examples and personal stories from my life. What I haven't covered is the after-life because this book is not supposed to be a "faith-based" book—that focus would turn away untold numbers of people who still need the "die neatly" financial philosophy.

However, I can't write about my life without closing with my Christian faith. If you've found what I've said in the prior chapters to be helpful, then I'd ask you to hear me out one last time because it's my faith that has shaped my belief system and led me to this concept of "dying neatly."

Naturally, you are very welcome to disagree with my faith views. I simply ask you to respect my faith, just like I should respect your own faith (or whatever beliefs you have freely come to follow). For me, it's from my faith that

I've achieved peace of mind as I live out the rest of my life, however long it may be until I reach my own "inevitable occurrence" of death.

In order for me to "die neatly" I have to have my family taken care of, and financially I don't want to become a liability before my death. Likewise, upon my death my wife Debbie will never have to worry about money, my grandchildren (and hopefully great grandchildren) will have college or professional training paid for, and my daughters will get substantial cash "love letters" delivered to them annually (which I hope they spend wisely). I also will ensure 10% of my estate goes to Christian (and other) philanthropy organizations, as per my faith beliefs (see Chapter 10: Legacy Planning).

This is all great and took a lot of planning, and I try to take care of myself to ensure I live many more years. I'm conscientious of my need to "slow down" both my driving and hard-charging lifestyle and try to take better care of myself. I do avoid the big vices, but I'm not in perfect health and am on some medication (as is common in my age group). I'm always trying to lose weight and exercise more, but like most people I procrastinate. So, in truth, I could die of a heart attack tomorrow (any of us could!) or live 25+ more years.

Therefore, despite my planning and attempts at self-care, how does my faith impact me, personally? My faith gives me strength and peace of mind through my belief that I will spend eternal life in Heaven with my Lord and Savior Jesus Christ, for which I'm grateful every day. My "die neatly" has to do with planning for everyone else because God has planned abundantly for me. Just as I desire to bless those I love through planning, God tells us about His planning in John 3:16: "For God so loved the world that He gave His only begotten Son [Jesus Christ] that whoever believes on Him shall not perish but have everlasting life."

I passionately believe that it's so important for you think of your own "after-life planning." Does your faith help you "die neatly?" If there is such a thing as eternal life, think about what it would be worth! We've talked about multi-million-dollar life insurance policies and the thousands of dollars they cost every month to keep active. Faith is much like taking out a life insurance policy. You simply have to sign up with God for His "after-life planning" program, but God loves us all so much that He doesn't charge us any premiums!

Instead of your money, God wants you to choose to have a relationship with Him, to give Him your heart and soul. Let me say again: this arrangement is offered freely. I can't earn it, and no one else can. Eternal life (being saved from sin) is a gift from Jesus who died for me and you and every person who believes in Him.

Let me close this faith section by explaining how my faith enables me to plan well, have peace of mind, and love others. You've already read my passionate beliefs about building a great "defensive financial plan" for my family. I want to be as prepared as possible for all kinds of catastrophic losses, and what is the most catastrophic loss of all? Ultimately, I believe the most catastrophic loss of all, even beyond death, is the death of our souls.

People say I'm an optimist and always happy. I do believe this is true of me (most of the time) but not because of what I've done. Granted, I have peace of mind through wise financial planning, such as my decision to own so much life insurance and long-term care insurance, but the *truly* long-term (eternal) care plan I put my faith in is salvation in Christ. It's this faith that has led me to have peace of mind about my life and family here on earth and my after-life. I believe my heart and mind are gifts from God, and I want to use them for His glory. I'm far from perfect, but I trust in my perfect, forgiving God.

So, going back to how we began the book with my "philosophy of three," I "hope for the best" through my faith in Christ. I "prepare for the worst" through wise Defensive Financial Planning. Lastly, I "take what comes" by living every day with love for others that starts with love for

God. This love then extends to my family, which I feel so blessed to have. Then it goes to my many friends and clients, and this love finally outpours to the world at large through charity work. This, to me, is how my faith enables me to "die neatly."

In other words, when death finally takes me, I pray that I'll go quickly without much suffering and my "inevitable occurrence" happens decades from now at age 100 (hope for the best!). However, even if I suffer for His Kingdom or die much sooner, I know I'm ready for my after-life because of God's gift of salvation (prepare for the worst...). Ultimately, I can rest in God's will, not mine, being done because I know God has reserved my place with Him for eternity (take what comes with gratitude!).

By the way, those of you who believe like me or are God-fearing people, please don't fall into the trap of not planning because "God will provide." God *has* provided you this very book to educate and motivate you to make use of His provision through wise planning. Jesus, himself, said "it is the foolish man who doesn't prepare for the storms of life and we are to be as wise builders.[10] So put your faith into practice so you can live for God and "die neatly!"

---

[10] Matthew 7:24-27. The Holy Bible.

I truly hope you take the time to carefully consider the right financial (and faith) choices for your life. In courageously confronting the reality of death you can remove much of the stress. It's inevitable, but it doesn't have to be a mess. Life insurance lets you deliver your "last love letter" to those so precious to you. With disability and long-term care insurance, you protect your Human Life Value, avoid erosion of your assets, and enable your family to have freedom from heavy burdens. With committed personal faith, you can plan beyond this life and into the next.

Thank you so much for reading this book, and God bless you all. Let me know if you are changed and motivated by it. Ultimately, when your time is finally up living here on earth, I want you to be able to say you have done all you could to truly "die neatly."

Jim Lusk, CFP®, CLU®, ChFC®, CLF, MEd
jim@retirementnationwide.com
www.retirementnationwide.com

www.LifeHappens.org
www.SSA.gov
www.ThePowerOfZeroBook.com
The Holy Bible (www.Bible.com)

ACKNOWLEDGMENTS

Thanks, go to Nick McCaskey, who did at least 14 edits of this book, to rephrase, spell check, grammar check, pray with me and try to understand what I'm trying to convey. I couldn't do this without you. Thanks also to Noland Peterdy, JD, MBA, PharmD and NPTG, brilliant man, friend, partner in my business, and his wife, Dr Geraldine, who did the best editing EVER.

Thanks to my "book coach" Andy Garrison and Coach Mike Burt for making this happen!

My deepest thanks to my early mentor and friend, Jim Bockemuehl. His sincere plea of "don't be hypocritical" has stuck with me to this very day. Thank you, Jim, for leading me in the path of integrity, needs based selling and "clients first."

A tremendous thank you to my mentor, Marty Polhemus (deceased), who was a former General Agent of Northwestern Mutual Life Insurance Company. Not only was he one of the greatest life insurance general agents ever, but he imparted tremendous wisdom directly to me. I give full credit to him for the three human life value stories I share in Chapter 5 (Cash Suitcase Buyout, The Money Machine, and Attorney from Ohio).

I'd like to thank Don Morgan, president of Independent Wealth Connections. Besides being my friend and business partner in many ways, he's an amazing connector of people. He's also a really great "offensive coordinator," and he's evolving into a great "defensive coordinator," too!

Thank you to my mentor, Virginia Faust, who was the director of the Washington State Teacher's Retirement System. Her conviction to pre-retirement planning and one of the best phrases I've ever used (go to www.retirementnationwide.com) has changed my life...

Thanks to Bill Simms for the testimonial at the end of Chapter 3.

Thank you to Ed VanVliet, Bob Bishopp, Paul Hanson and the rest of the NML family

Thanks to New York Life and many friends and mentors there for the awesome career I had with them for 22 years and the many convictions, processes and teaching tools that I learned there.

Thanks to Ameritas Life Insurance company, specifically David Richert, for contracting my General Agency and the opportunity to continue to recruit, train, and develop agents with this great company, as well as awesome products to serve our clients. Thanks also to the A-Team for trusting my leadership and following the process.

Thank you Harry Amend, a long-time friend, mentor, coach, leader, and FCA director in 1971 when I found Christ. You've been there for me my whole life since then. I love you my brother!

Thank you to Bob Theichart, my performance coach for 15 years. Where would I be without you, Bob? You've taken on so many roles (teacher, coach, shrink) to help me and still are!

Thank you to my wonderful friends and clients for trusting me for guidance over all the years.

Thank you to my whole family for inspiring so much through the years. Thank you for allowing me to share some of your stories of hardship and perseverance. Thank you to my sister, Peggy, for supporting my business and being so consistently honest, buying into the firm and being the CFO...

Thank you, especially to my wife Debbie, for being my best friend, best critic, and loving motivator. I love you so much since 1974! You mothered Jaimie and Jodi with such grace and care, and now: Tom, Dinah, Ezekiel and Enoch. Where would my life be without this precious family?

Most of all, thank you God for giving me the amazing blessing of a healthy life, an incredible wife, two beautiful and
smart daughters, and the most awesome grandchildren I
could ever want. Thank you for assuring me of a mind-
blowing after-life through my faith in your Son, Jesus
Christ!

APPENDIX

The following resources have been gathered from 37 years of meetings, workshops, speakers, and copious note-taking.

1. Consumer Attitudes about Life Insurance

2. Power Phrases about Death

3. Power Phrases about Life Insurance

4. Power Phrases about Life Insurance Careers

5. Final Quotes

Exhibit 1 – Consumer Attitudes about Life Insurance

Anxiety – Caused by...

1. Unpleasant – Associated with death

2. Confusion – Ignorance of the product (conflicting and incomplete data and claims)

3. Mistrust – Thinks agent motives are impure ("Must sell to survive")

Other concerns:

1. Remoteness of the companies – Huge, untouchable, non-responsive

2. Big money involved

3. Premium payments go on and on – For their "whole life"

But the truth is:

1. Life insurance is important and necessary

2. Once they understand it, they appreciate it

3. Once they own it, they have a "peace of mind"

Exhibit 2 – Power Phrases about Death

The day you die is the most expensive day of your life.

When you die, Mr. Prospect, there will be three deaths: a husband/wife, a father/mother, and an income.

One of two things is certain tomorrow—either you will die or you will live.

The reason clients insure is not because they are afraid they may die, but because they know their families must live.

The high cost of living cannot be compared with the high cost of dying. Who do you want to pay—your family or your life insurance company?

You either have an estate "tax" problem or an estate "size" problem.

Consider a man who takes his family's life savings and disappears leaving behind his wife and little daughter with nothing. You and I would never do that, but what is the financial difference between him and the man who dies leaving his family in the same monetary situation?

How much are your tomorrows worth?

Man is under a sentence of death—the only question is, when will the sentence be carried out?

If it makes sense to pay 1% to manage money, doesn't it make sense to pay 1% to create the right amount of money at death?

The death rate of investments is greater than the death rate of men. More of my prospects go broke before they die than die before they go broke.

How long can your family go without your paycheck?

A businessman may take plenty of risks in his or her career, but a gamble on untimely death need not be one of them.

The more you are worth, the more your dependents stand to lose. The less you are worth, the less they can afford to lose.

The worst time for a homemaker to become a wage earner is when he becomes a widower, or she becomes a widow.

Are you giving your family the benefit of the same good business judgement the court would compel you to give were you handling the affairs of another?

Your first duty to your children is not to leave them a large amount of money but rather to make sure that Dad and Mom will never be dependent upon them.

You are your family's trustee. The question is, are you a good trustee?

Mistaken kindness—to provide so well today that there is no provision for tomorrow.

Some people are so prosperous today that their purchasing power is just a little better than their judgement.

One father out of five will not live to see his child through college.

Mr. Prospect, I think you will agree with me that motherhood is a full-time job.

It is far easier to pay for a college education over ten or fifteen years than in four.

Exhibit 3 – Power Phrases about Life Insurance

Will Rogers said, "If a man doesn't believe in life insurance, let him die once without it. That will teach him a lesson!"

You can repent in the "eleventh hour," but you seldom can buy life insurance then.

Your widow's or widower's most cherished memories of your good intentions will not pay the rent or the grocer's bill. A good life insurance plan turns good intentions into great certainties.

Not to insure adequately is the greatest gamble a man can take, and it is a particularly mean one, for if he loses, it is his family who pays.

Why isn't it logical to insure your lifetime earning power in the true amount of your family's insurable interest?

If it is difficult for you to raise 2% or 3% today, Mr. Prospect, how could your family raise 100% tomorrow?

Your spouse will either have income provided for him or her or by him or her.

A husband or wife may object to life insurance, but a widower or widow never does.

Any of these excuses you give me now, Mr. Prospect, would sound silly to your widow, wouldn't they?

What arrangements have you made for your widow after the proceeds of your life insurance run out?

Life insurance is always paid for by sacrifices. Either you sacrifice a little now and obtain the coverage you need, or your family will have to sacrifice a great deal later because of the protection you did not provide for them.

"No one has a lease on life. If you don't die before you reach age 65, you will die after age 65. No one is promised tomorrow." – Ben Feldman

Insurance is like a parachute. You have to own it before you need it, and if you don't have it when you do need it, it's too late to get it.

How much will having life insurance realistically decrease your standard of living? Not having it could decrease your family's standard of living dramatically.

Life insurance is paid for whether you buy it or not. Either you can pay premiums for it today, or tomorrow your family will pay for it in terms of doing without.

The best time to buy life insurance is now. If you wait, your health may change or you might die. In any event, your age changes which means the cost will increase.

The premium is not the problem. The premium is the solution to the problem. Compared to the problem, the premium is peanuts.

Only two things in life are certain... death and taxes. Life insurance can help you take the sting out of both.

Life insurance is just a common sense recognition of reality.

Life and life insurance are about values.

Permanent life insurance costs you nothing—to not own it costs you everything.

Life insurance is a contract of "time and money." If suddenly your "time's up," we'll "pay up" so your family can "keep up" living.

Life insurance doesn't keep people from dying. It keeps their plans from dying with them.

We ensure that when you die, your debts die with you.

It's bad enough to die. Don't do it for free.

No insurance—"You don't plan on being dead too long, do you?"

Life insurance is the only investment you'll ever make that you are discriminated against by your age and your health.

Life insurance is the only insurance you'll own that you'll make money, even if the catastrophe doesn't happen.

Life insurance is a bad investment, but investments are bad life insurance.

You only need life insurance if you love someone else.

The day he/she "walks out the door," the money walks in, tax-free.

If you keep permanent life insurance until death, it costs you nothing.

"Term insurance is a great buy as long as you 'get lucky' and die young."

Term insurance is like wetting the bed... it gives you temporary relief but eventually you have to get up and do something about it.

The people who profess "buy term and invest the difference" probably don't have the difference.

People usually "buy term and enjoy the difference" rather than "buy term and invest the difference."

Exhibit 4 – Power Phrases about Life Insurance Careers

I help business owners decide whether they love the IRS or their family more.

I deliver "love letters" to widows and widowers.

If I can show you how to possibly become wealthy or guarantee that your family will never be poor, which would you do first?

I want to come to your funeral with a very large check and a clear conscious, knowing that your family is covered.

I don't have any old clients who wish that they had purchased less life insurance.

Clients want to know how much you care before they care how much you know.

Make the sale, develop a relationship, and then smother them with kindness.

Success is measured by the positive impact you've had on others.

Love doesn't last long with clients—be respected and loved.

Don't divert your great efforts and become a rookie in some other field.

Go for luxuries and the necessities will take care of themselves.

We are in the business of "selling capital."

I'm a financial dentist—no one likes the procedure, everyone likes the results.

No success in the field will compensate for a failure at home.

Exhibit 5 – Final Quotes

"It just seems to be some people's luck to get blamed for being good in their business. Well, you know how it is. If a guy is going to sell any insurance for instance, why, he's gotta kinda stick around and ask people if they don't want some more insurance. The crowd ain't going to walk all the way upstairs to his office and knock on the door to be led to buy a little insurance no matter how good it is. And then they poke lots of fun at their insurance agents for peddling their stuff. I like insurance agents myself, because they do more good than a lot of fellows that just sit around looking dignified." – Will Rogers

"I'm a life insurance salesman. Other salesmen are limited. They just sell furniture, appliances, or shoes. I sell these too. And I sell many thing more. I sell meat, bread, and milk for the table of a family deprived of a father. I sell cancelled mortgages so that mother and the children can live in comfortable, familiar surroundings. I sell college educations for youngsters, to give them better opportunities in life. I sell the little extras—ice cream cones, roller skates, a dress for the prom. I make life worth living. I sell golf clubs, fishing tackle, exciting trips, and self-respect for your later years. I sell all the necessities and good things of life, because life insurance is for the living. Yes, I am a life insurance salesman, and pardon me if my pride is showing." – Norman Dinwiddie

LIST OF DIAGRAMS

Chapter 4

DIAGRAM: Perception of Life Expectancy

DIAGRAM: Life Expectancy Chances

DIAGRAM: Bell Curve for Life Expectancy

Chapter 5

DIAGRAM: 9/11 Victims' Fund

DIAGRAM: Human Life Value (Earnings to Age 65)

DIAGRAM: Money Machine

Chapter 7

DIAGRAM: Life Insurance – Term versus Permanent (Curved Line vs Flat Line)

DIAGRAM: Life Insurance Retirement Portfolio (LIRP) Example

Chapter 10

DIAGRAM: "Tithing Your Estate" – 10% and 90%

Chapter 11

DIAGRAM: Disability insurance – Before and After a Disability

ABOUT THE AUTHOR

Jim Lusk started in the Life Insurance business in 1983 with Northwestern Mutual Life after teaching public high school math and physics for 6 years. He founded Retirement Nationwide, Inc. in 1985 after he obtained his securities license, paid for over 100 lives per year and qualified for MDRT every year. His focus was serving young families, retiring public employees and closely held private businesses, all three that he still serves and coaches others to serve today.

Jim was a fast track to management because of his desire and talent to teach and coach and spent 20 plus years as a first line manager with New York Life where he "retired" from in 2017 with a sweet lifetime pension. The next day, he switched his DBA to the president (again) of Retirement Nationwide, Inc. and reinvented the firm by recruiting, training, and developing advisors to become the premier Defensive Financial Planning firm in the nation.

Jim is married to Debbie, since 1976, when he was 21 and she was 19. Without her, he says he'd be a lost soul. They have two daughters, Jaimie and Jodi and three grandchildren. He plans to "never retire" and live the rest of his blessed life in Spokane, Washington. His goals are to continue to work hard teaching and training agents, play harder, love his friends and family, travel, give back time and money, golf a little, woodwork in his "man cave," and enjoy the rest of his life....all knowing that if he dies too soon and/or needs long-term care, his plan for his family and charities is to not leave a mess. His plan is to "die neatly."

Made in the USA
Monee, IL
16 April 2021